MARK WEIGHTON

CHANGING FACE AND FACES

Photograph by Jim and Eileen Wilson

ENID M. GREENWOOD

Highgate of Beverley

Highgate Publications (Beverley) Limited
2000

IN MEMORY OF TOM

Front Cover: Top: Southgate, about 1910.
Below: Northgate, looking towards the Market Hill.

Title Page: Aerial view of Market Weighton, 1994.

British Library Cataloguing in Publication Data.
A catalogue record for this book is available from the British Library.

© 2000 Enid M. Greenwood
Enid M. Greenwood asserts the moral right to be identified as the author of this work.

ISBN 1 902645 13 8

Published by

Highgate of Beverley

Highgate Publications (Beverley) Limited
4 Newbegin, Beverley, HU17 8EG. Telephone (01482) 886017

Produced by

ba/print

4 Newbegin, Beverley, HU17 8EG. Telephone (01482) 886017

EARLY REMEMBRANCES

It was in May 1928 that I was born in my mother and father's bedroom in our family home. This was adjoining and above the family grocer's shop in a narrow street known as Market Place. It was situated at the centre of a little market town called Market Weighton, in the East Riding of Yorkshire, which was to play a very big part in most of my life.

My father, Harold William Lyon, was born in the same house too, and then he went to live in the shop house with his wife, Kate Brigham, in 1919 after their wedding at Knaresborough Methodist Chapel. My grandfather retired to Tryste House, a Georgian house built in 1791, in Finkle Street. My parents had met in Market Weighton when my mother lived at Wold House, a farm up the hill off the Beverley Road. They both went to the Wesleyan Chapel and attended parties at the Sunday School there. This building was the old chapel of 1786 where John Wesley had once preached.

When I lived at the shop premises the main street was quiet compared with today, and there were very few cars. On market day, a Wednesday, there were stalls on the road opposite the shop. The farmers stood outside the Londesborough Arms, and inside I should think, selling their crops and discussing business. The farmers' wives would sell their butter and eggs and buy their food and household goods. I am told that my Grandmother Brigham was proud that her butter was considered the second best that my Grandfather Lyon bought to sell in the shop. Just inside the back door of the house was an egg candler where eggs brought in by farmers' wives were tested before being sold in the shop. Hens on farms often lay away and the eggs collected may not be fresh.

I have also been told that some of the farmers' wives sold their produce while standing near the

My mother and father are at the back on the left.

Wold House where my mother lived. Since demolished.

shop yard, with their baskets at their feet. In these would be dressed poultry as well as the butter and eggs. The money they made would be their housekeeping money, but the husband would pay for the food for the hens and other animals.

My early life at the shop was made even happier because of a family who were ironmongers and lived on the other side of the street. Mr. and Mrs. Potter, Ethel their daughter, and Mr. Potter's mother lived above and below the shop, in conditions that were far from easy. Down in the cellar, which was below the level of the graves in the churchyard behind, was the kitchen. The stairs from there were steep and narrow and came up into the back of the shop and then up to the living room. This was the same size as the shop, and immediately above it. A further flight of stairs went up from the end of the room to the two bedrooms. The stairs came straight into one room, which is where 'Granny

1932. Market Day outside Londesborough Arms.

Potter' slept. In one corner of her room was a lavatory. Mr. and Mrs. Potter and Ethel slept in the next room, having to go through the bedroom where the old woman was sleeping. Ethel had to sleep with her mother and father until her grandmother died. These conditions were not unusual in those days and some were far worse where big families lived in tiny cottages and many children slept in the same bed.

In the shop were all kinds of ironmongery including tin baths and buckets hanging from the ceiling. Paraffin at 1s. a gallon, candles, oil lamps, lamp glasses and wicks and many other articles were sold, On market day Mr. Potter had a stall outside on the road selling trunks that farm workers used when moving from farm to farm. He had a tall desk where he stood to write up his books.

Another shop that interested me was approached by steep steps. This was a favourite because it sold 'farmyard'. I avidly collected these little lead animals and people, and would go in to Ladley's shop grasping my penny pocket money and peering round to find the choice piece of the week. I would sometimes go to Wilson's stationer's and toy shop on the corner of Londesborough Road. Here each different piece was in a small partition that formed a stack of small wooden boxes at the back of the shop. Another way of obtaining these farmyard pieces was in packets of cornflakes of a variety not seen today called Farmer's Glory. No other cornflakes tasted quite so good to me.

The little chemist shop next door to ours had a beautiful bow window that is now in the Castle Museum at York. It belonged to Mr. and Mrs. Masterman and their daughter, Elsie. They were a gentle,

kind family and very good neighbours. One of their daughters had tuberculosis, and a summer house was made which could be easily turned round to face the sun.

The ironmonger's to the west of our shop, S. H. Cooper and Son, belonged to my father's uncle, and the next shop, which was still part of the same premises, was a draper's, belonging at that time to Charles Stather. When my grandparents were at the shop my father used to say that you could take any

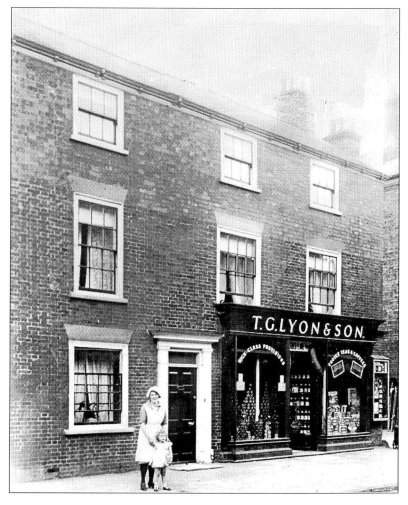

When I was two. Standing outside the shop.

two people from the three shops and they were cousins. All three men married their cousins and all were cousins to each other. All the couples 'lived above the shop' as was usual at that time.

At the bottom of our yard was a door which is still there in 1999. It led to a very long garden. Just through the door were Victoria plum trees which, when I was a child, were very old, but they gave us baskets full of beautiful plums. After that came the raspberry canes, again very prolific. Beyond this was the lawn with a summer house in one corner. Most of our activities as children took place on that lawn.

Next was the vegetable garden, but the part which was most thrilling to me was at the very bottom of the garden. A brick wall ran right across the end and, if I stood on a box, I could look over to gaze across the fields (now Scott's Croft and other houses) and look down into the beck. My sisters, who were older than me, could hang over the wall but I had to stand on the box in order to see over it.

Further up stream was a carrot-washing plant; the area is now called Massey's Corner. The tiny carrots escaped down stream, and our favourite game was to hang over the wall with a long string with a jam jar fastened to it. The prize was to catch a carrot in the jar. These were collected up and eaten, but sometimes my sisters would 'cook' them on the manure heap. They would make a choice of orange, raspberry or lemon drink which was not very appetising as it was made from coloured crepe paper squeezed out in water. My sisters gave it to a second cousin who used to come from Bradford to stay with his grandparents next door. He seems to have survived the ordeal.

Another favourite game was hide and seek in the buildings and on the lorries when the shop was closed. We all learnt to ride a bicycle on the cobbles in the yard. We liked to go down the passage of the upstairs warehouse and weigh ourselves on the big scales used for sacks of animal foods. My mother told how she went down with my father and his sisters, before she was married, on a Sunday and how frightened she was when they suggested being weighed. She was very strictly brought up and her father would not do anything on the Sabbath. We used to go down to feed the cats that were there to keep down the mice. A call of 'Puss, puss, puss!' would bring cats scuttling from all directions.

Another fascinating place was the treacle room. Large barrels, standing on trestles, were full of golden syrup and black treacle. Each had a tap on the front under which stood a small bucket to catch the drips. It was easy to dip into the bucket with a little finger and scoop up some treacle to a mouth waiting open to suck it.

Before my time, there were horses in the stables and wagons waiting down the yard. There was a building at the bottom of the yard in which was a generator which made the electricity for the house and shop. Our premises were one of the first to have electricity in Market Weighton. Our washing was done in the wash house, which was nearly at the bottom of the yard, and the clothes were hung out in the garden beyond. It must have been difficult if there was a heavy shower while the washing was out. We had a washerwoman to do the washing, but, before she could start, the copper had to be lit. This not only heated the water to put in the dolly tub and washing tub, but boiled the whites as well. A little fire underneath was fuelled with waste wood and cardboard and maybe a little coal.

Each Sunday morning we put on our best clothes and went to chapel. I remember wearing a straw hat with a wide brim with pretty little flowers round it, a summer dress and white socks and gloves. We had a family pew which was just two from the front at the St. John's Wesleyan chapel built in 1868. We shared it with Grandpa and Granny Lyon and our aunts. This pew was the only one with a little cupboard in which to keep hymn books and my grandfather's bible. I liked to sit next to him as he sucked little violet sweets and he would give one to me if I was sitting next to him. In the pew in front was a lady who always came in late. As she was rather a large person and always wore very elaborate hats, her sudden presence caused great amusement to us. Her hats were decorated with birds, fruit and flowers and looked as though she was about to take off and fly.

The minister gave the children a talk and then, before the sermon started, all the children went out to the Sunday School room. This was under an arch in the old Methodist chapel, which is the oldest chapel still standing in the East Riding but now the home of an upholstery firm. We sang songs and hymns to the accompaniment of my Auntie Annie, on a rather ancient piano on the stage. We sat on forms and occasionally were allowed to march round these to the music. Then we had a story and received a coloured card decorated with a bible picture. By this time our mothers and fathers were coming out of chapel to collect us.

My family have had a very long association with Market Weighton and I have been lucky that some of them were 'hoarders' and kept

Our pew

X

Taken from the choir

Our pew in the chapel.

documents and photographs from the past. Another family which also kept many photographs is the Parkinson's, and fortunately Mr. John Wreggitt has saved these from destruction.

I found that I could not write about Market Weighton in an impersonal way and have also had to include rather a large amount about some of my ancestors, but they were very much part of the life. To the serious historian I do apologise. This book is written about the people of this town, for them and anyone interested in it. It is not intended as an architectural view of Market Weighton as there are people far more qualified to write about this than I am. It is more a social history, mainly of the last 150 years, intended to show the newer residents what life was like and to give old 'Weightonians' a chance to reminisce and find all the things that I didn't know, and hopefully some which they didn't know either.

I have tried very hard to be accurate and sometimes have had to leave facts out that people have told me if they could not be proved. Memories sometimes become exaggerated over the years.

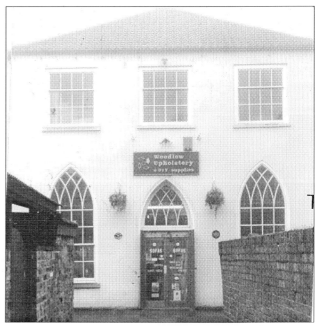

The old chapel became the Sunday School.

AN AERIAL PHOTOGRAPH TAKEN IN 1938 SHOWING THE EAST END OF THE TOWN

A   Old Oddfellows Hall. This part of it is now demolished and is a car park and garden.

B   The Central Cinema. Now demolished and is a car park.

C   The old lodging house. Now demolished and is a car park.

D   Leakes fold yard. Now demolished and is replaced by the houses on Hill Rise.

E   The Red Lion public house.

F   The old Georgian cinema house which had been the Bridge Hotel. Now demolished.

G   This little street is The Arch. All the cottages shown have been demolished.

H   Finkle Street.

J   This is Tryste House on Finkle Street. It is a Georgian house now made into flats.

K   The old police station and Court house. It became a police house. Now a private house.

L   The old brewery. Now demolished and has been replaced by flats.

M   The old fire station.

N   Now called Massey's Corner. There were houses on the corner until Robert B Massey's garage was built, when they were demolished . Now shops and a restaurant.

O   The Green.

MARKET WEIGHTON AS IT WAS

All Saints Church is situated in the very centre of the town, as it should be. It is a pity that over the early years the people who had stalls in the Market Place decided to build shops instead and so spoilt what would have been a lovely view of the church.

During the Second World War all but one of these premises was unoccupied and used only for troops stationed in the town. A suggestion was made that the shops should be demolished and the area be landscaped to widen the road and give a better view of the church. This, however, did not materialise and many properties of much greater importance architecturally were later demolished.

Market Weighton church exterior

The church, which has a small part dating from the 11th century, was mainly built in the Early English and Perpendicular styles. It had, until 1785, a wooden spire on top of the tower but was then finished with the present-day brick tower which we all associate with Market Weighton. I found a bill in 1826 which was for tolling the bell for the Duke of York's funeral – four shillings.

In January 1869 at a meeting of the Church Council held at the infant school in Hungate it was decided that vast changes were needed to the church.

The following was reported in the minutes of that meeting:

> 'That it is desirable to remove the galleries and other obstructions from the Parish Church and reseat the floor in a uniform and substantial manner, also introduce new heating apparatus and make the necessary alteration to the gas fittings at an expected cost of £600.'

In 1871 the north aisle was rebuilt and the nave section of the aisle enlarged. New roofing was placed on the whole church and the nave and aisles were reseated. A new east window was constructed in the same year. The chancel roof and window were designed by Lord Londesborough's Clerk of Works but the architects for the rest of the work were Messrs. Atkinson of York.

The cost of the work on the chancel was defrayed by Lord Londesborough and the money for the rest was collected partly by subscription, helped by a grant from the Diocesan Church Building Society and partly by a mortgage on the Church Estate for £500 repayable in equal yearly instalments, twelve in number. The chancel stalls were new in 1860.

The church was re-opened in October 1871. There were two services at the re-opening of the church and each time it was full:

> 'Between the two services the archbishop, clergy, churchwardens (Messrs. Consitt and Mitchell) and other friends were entertained at an elegant and sumptuous luncheon provided solely by Mrs. Samuel Botterill of Manor House Farm in the Temperance Hall. The room was decorated by Messrs. Richardson and Towse and great credit was due to them for the beauty of the decorations. The walls were covered with appropriate designs.'

Unfortunately at the evening service, due to unforeseen circumstances, there was no gas to light the church and paraffin lamps had to be substituted.

An organ by Ward of York, a fine instrument with two rows of manuals and an octave of pedals was purchased from the late Rev. William Blow of Goodmanham and placed in Market Weighton church in 1860 but in 1883 a new organ made by Jones and Sons of Kensington was bought. The clock was installed in 1832. The floor of the chancel was finished in black and white marble to commemorate Queen Victoria's Diamond Jubilee in 1897.

In 1967 Mr. Charles Frankish and the vicar thought it very proper that

Flower festival 1998.

the bell should be tolled at the passing of a parishioner's soul, so that our people might know and offer a prayer. After 'nine tailors' for a man and the 'six maidens' for a woman, the age of the person is tolled.

In 1978 the clock on the church tower was very much missed by many people – but the repairs had to be paid for before it could come back. £12,000 was needed before the clock would be returned and the bells could ring.

The old Wesleyan Methodist Chapel of 1786 is the oldest surviving one in the East Riding and noteworthy also as John Wesley preached there in 1788. He said:

'At eleven I preached, with much enlargement of heart, in the new chapel at Market Weighton.'

The chapel seating plan drawn by William Watson shows what it was like inside. It closed as a chapel in 1868 when a new, larger chapel, designed by William Botterill of Hull, was opened. The old one became the Sunday School and Chapel hall. The foundation stone for the new chapel was laid in July 1868. Afterwards a tea was held over two days and large numbers of people enjoyed the occasion.

Once the chapel had been built, at a cost of £1,600, the

Church scaffolded, 1908.

General Booth's visit, 1907.

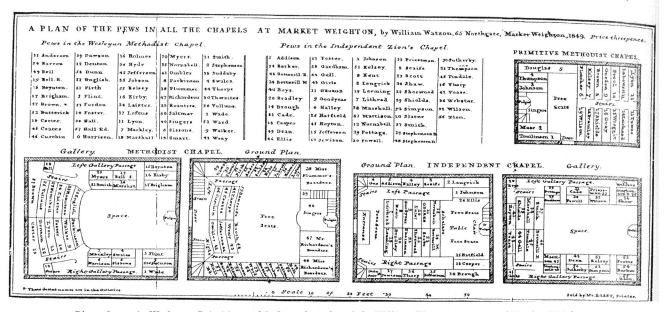

Plan of pews in Wesleyan, Primitive and Independent chapels by William Watson, surveyor of Market Weighton.
It shows the seating and membership of all the nonconformist chapels in 1849.

St. John's Methodist Chapel.

Bruce Miles playing chapel organ.

Methodist Hall, 1997.

The organ in St. Johns Methodist Chapel, erected 1878.

opening on Thursday, 1 October 1868, was an even greater occasion. Some of the shops were closed to enable the owners and staff to attend the services and people also came by train. Evidently at that time the goods trains had attached to them a passenger carriage and these were used by the visitors.

The chapel was full, with people even standing in the aisles, and the opening was performed and the service taken by Rev. S. Romilly Hall, who was at that time the President of the Methodist Conference.

The tea afterwards was described by local reporters with great enthusiasm:

'It certainly has not befallen our lot to witness such a tea meeting before, for from four o'clock to six in the evening no less than seven hundred people took tea.'

Then the crowds with their appetites thoroughly satisfied went on to another service at 6.30, in the chapel. A congregation of about 900 was present. Again the President spoke, followed by Rev. Thomas Wray, who was 84 years old. He said that he had been converted about 70 years before in the old chapel.

The chapel bazaars were held in the school-room and, although possibly held only every third year, entailed a great deal of work for the ladies. I can remember my grandmother feverishly making garments, and beautiful tablecloths were edged with crochet work. The occasion lasted for two days and was held in the upstairs room (now filled with chairs and sofas). Wonderful teas were served downstairs. The kitchen is now the upholstery shop. A great deal of money was made at these bazaars.

The first Methodist Manse, taken about 1900.
Hannah Rushby with milk can.

7

Tryste House, pre-1919.

TRYSTE HOUSE on Finkle Street has on its rainwater heads the date of 1791. It is considered by David Neave to be the best surviving house of the 18th century in the town. A smaller house on the other side of Finkle Street was built in the same period. Tryste House has many memories for me as in 1919 my grandfather, Thomas G. Lyon, bought it and lived there until he died in 1946. I remember being taken there every Sunday afternoon. The garden was very long and went all the way up to the garden of Givendale Lodge. My grandfather was a very keen gardener and also employed a man and a boy, who would learn a great deal about gardening. In 1937 Rev. G. Bramwell Evans, better known to children at that time as Romany of BBC children's programmes, came to preach at the chapel and was entertained at Tryste House. He wrote in one of his books about the garden there.

Later the house was the home of Wicstun Junior High School, better known as Miss Penty's, which had moved from smaller premises on the corner of Holme Road and Linegate. Our two daughters were very ably

taught by her in their early years, and it was strange to realise that their classroom had been my grandfather's bedroom and the little washbasin in the corner of their cloakroom was the self-same one where my grandmother had washed my hands as a tiny child, soaping her own hands and rubbing mine with them.

The large garden was no longer there now, but even more strange is the fact that one of my daughters has a house built on what had been my grandfather's orchard. It is in the road called Manor Fields. Tryste House is now converted into flats and bed-sitting rooms.

THE MARKET WEIGHTON AND ARRAS WAR MEMORIAL INSTITUTE

The following article was found in an old newspaper dated May 1919. It said:

'War Memorial Concert – The War Memorial Committee presided over by Councillor Thomas G. Lyon J.P. on Tuesday evening last in The Oddfellows Hall explained the proposal to raise £2,000 to build and provide a non-sectarian Town's Institute as a useful and suitable war memorial. The adult inhabitants were invited by free tickets to a most enjoyable vocal and instrumental concert provided by Mr. John Metcalfe and his party. An encouraging address

The Institute, 1997.

Top right: The Institute. Behind it the gas works manager's house.

Thomas Lyon gardening.

The interior of the Institute, 1997.

was given by Rev. Father Wright. A voluntary collection towards expenses realised £7. 14s. A vote of thanks was given to the artists for their services. Councillor Lyon (chairman) explained that close on £200 had already been raised, £100 given by himself for the safe return of his son, £50 by Mr. S. T Cockburn and £43 raised by the Town Band. The chairman offered to give an additional £50 and provide the last £100 to complete the £2,000 required for the scheme.'

When my father went to the First World War, my grandfather put away sixpence for every day his son was away and gave the money for the Institute. The club was intended as a place for men to play billiards and read the newspapers, but in the twenties Ivan Medforth's father introduced snooker to the town and there are now three snooker tables. At one time there was also a library. A bar, later introduced, made the hall more popular, and the club, with a licence to serve alcoholic drinks for the Carlsberg Tetley Brewery, is run by the Market Weighton and Arras War Memorial Institute Committee.

It has, on the outside, a plaque at each side of the door inscribed with the names of 57 servicemen who fell in the First World War and 17 people who were killed in the Second World War. The British Legion pay homage there to the fallen of both wars every year on Remembrance Day.

THE FLORAL HALL

The building on Holme Road now used by Pieter Plantenga as a pine warehouse was known as the Floral Hall when I was young. It was built on land belonging to Mrs. Annie Cockburn in about 1921. It was used by Mr. Cockburn for storing wool which he bought from local farmers, but later became a hall, being used mainly for boxing bouts:

'The Boxing contests held in the Floral Hall last Monday night were poorly attended. Some very interesting bouts were well worthy of better support.'

There were also reports in the newspaper in 1935 of the annual general meeting of the tennis club presided over by Mr. Cockburn. and also meetings of the Conservative Association. In 1937 it had been leased by Mr. Clifford Sugden for storing hessian potato sacks. When any came back dirty they were washed and hung across to dry. Mr. Sugden and Derek, his son, had their office in the old cloakrooms, and even then the electricity bill always came addressed to 'The Floral Hall'. Once when their offices were there they found a ticket for a dance, price 1s. 6d., and Pieter Plantenga found boxing gloves on the false roof of the office. During the war it became the headquarters of the Home Guard.

I remember going to a children's party there when it was still the Floral Hall. I believe several families hired it for this purpose. It was a much better building than the Oddfellows Hall with a stage at the far end, but it never seemed to be so popular, possibly because it was not so central.

So many of these old buildings have now disappeared, including what was locally called The Brewery but was in fact a maltings. This was designed by William Hawe of Driffield, who also designed the Victorian house which used to be called The Hollies. This is now St. Catherine's Nursing Home on Londesborough Road, built in 1876, a year later than the Maltings. William Hawe also designed houses on York Road and Southgate in 1887. It is also possible that the building now used as a post office, and HSBC and others on Holme Road were thought to have been designed by him.

The building which was the Floral Hall.

The brewery is down, 1991. Looking from the Green.

The old Floral Hall in 1997.

Market Weighton 150 years ago

The Old King's Arms, 1848

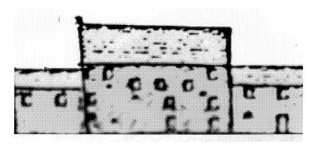

The tannery on Finkle Street, which became the Oddfellows Hall.

Temperance Hall   *Temperance Hotel*

Market Place, Market Weighton, 1848

William Cade's windmill. Situated near Londesborough Road, 1848.

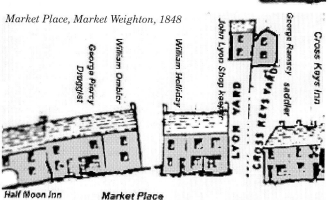

The first Primitive Methodist Chapel, Beverley Road, Market Weighton, 1848

Board Inn or Bridge House, 1848

The old Police Station and Court House, The Green, 1848

Illustrations taken from William Watson's map of 1848.

THE LOST BUILDINGS

I had forgotten how many buildings and features had disappeared in Market Weighton even in the last 50 years until I started thinking about it. There have been few changes in the main street but in some roads there have been many buildings demolished, particularly Southgate and Northgate, which has even changed its name to York Road. Hungate has had two changes of name, to Dalton Road and now to Spring Road. Hawling Road was known locally as Sweep Lane.

ODDFELLOWS HALL

The first building which comes to mind was situated in Finkle Street, which runs north from the mini roundabout at the end of the High Street, and is the road to Kiplingcotes and Dalton. The Oddfellows Hall is one of the old buildings of Market Weighton which has disappeared. It was very well known at one time but not many present-day inhabitants of Market Weighton have even heard of it. I found it impossible to find a photograph of it taken from Finkle Street, but the aerial photograph of 1938 shows it. I was very lucky to be able to study the deeds which John Moore, the blacksmith and present owner of a small part of the building, lent me during a snowy week one winter. Some were beautifully written on large sheets of parchment. It has a very complicated history, having changed hands many times.

Part of the old Oddfellows Hall, Finkle Street. Now the blacksmith's shop.

John and Nicholas Moore, the blacksmiths and farriers.

The first information was in the very early 18th century when it was described as a tannery, occupied by Henry Gray Dales, a tanner. In 1801 Robert Wilson, another tanner, bought the property, and in the sale, which amounted to £800, was included tan-yard buildings, tan tubs and fixtures. In 1830 Robert Wilson died and his son, Robert Wilson junior, took it over. Unfortunately in 1833 he was made bankrupt and it was put up for sale by public auction at the Beverley Arms Inn, and bought by Edward Carter, who lived at Market Weighton but later moved to Howden. He must have retired then, as in 1861 its use was changed to that of a brewery when it was bought by Robert Jewison, brewer and wine merchant. In 1879 its use changed again to that of a steam corn mill when it was sold to Israel Kelsey, corn miller and farmer, and Thomas Scott, corn miller, both of Market Weighton. In 1881 it was worth £2,000. It included the engine, boiler, machinery and fixtures. After the death of George Scott senior it passed to his son, George, who was under 21, and his trustees were Thomas Jewison Jefferson, doctor of medicine at Market Weighton, Richard Simpson, brewer, and Elizabeth Simpson, widow of George Scott, all of this town. In 1902 when the property was sold to Samuel Brough, a mineral water manufacturer, it was described as a 'Disused corn mill together with the messuage or dwelling house, warehouse, drying kiln, stable, granaries, piggeries, office and other buildings'.

I found an advertisement dated 1904 for the sale of Hackney House only, by Samuel Sharp, auctioneer, at the Londesborough Arms Hotel. It announced the sale of a freehold messuage or dwelling-house known as Hackney House situate in Finkle Street together with stables, yard, garden, outbuildings, conveniences and appurtenances belonging and recently in the occupation of Mr. J. W. Murgatroyd. It also stated that it had water and gas laid on and contained three excellent sitting-rooms, large kitchen, five bedrooms, pantry, wash-house, WC and ample out offices, but there was no mention of a disused corn mill.

It then passed into the hands of Mr. Robert Morley, threshing machine proprietor, who must have bought it at the auction, but in 1914 it went into the ownership of Gildon Wilson, a farmer of High Meltham Farm, Eastrington. At this time the sale notice gave the name of the property as 'Oddfellows Hall'. It said that the house, which was adjoining, known as Hackney House, and some of the buildings were in the occupation of Walker Layton. This was in 1914, but in 1918 it was sold to Herbert Hornsey, auctioneer of Market Weighton, who moved into Hackney House. There were other owners after this until it was bought in 1983 by Moore brothers, the blacksmiths, who still carry on business in the part which has not been demolished.

Looking at old newspapers I wanted to find when it became used as a hall for the people of Market Weighton. The first time it was mentioned was for a poultry show in January 1903 when the *Howdenshire Gazette* reported:

'Had these gentlemen been able to announce that the show would be held in Market Weighton town hall instead of Mr. Morley`s engine room, they could confidently expect a largely increased attendance.'

In spite of this many more poultry shows were later held there and these included farm produce such as butter.

Referring to other activities I have an article about a presentation to Dr. Jefferson for completing 45 years as medical officer. The address was given by Dr. Ashwin at a gathering of the Loyal Maxwell Lodge of Oddfellows. Thereafter the upstairs of the building was always known locally as the Oddfellows Hall and became a very popular place in the social life of Market Weighton, yet this was the only time I could find the Oddfellows Lodge mentioned in the newspapers.

There were endless dances, some in aid of the football club, children's fancy dress competitions, fancy dress balls and concerts by the new town brass band.

In 1904: MARKET WEIGHTON BRASS BAND
'The public in and around Market Weighton are delighted with the progress the Town Band have made of late. The band are expecting their new uniform this week-end and have already got several engagements for clubs, feasts, shows etc. and are prepared to accept others. Applications may be made to Mr. R. Layton, hon. sec.'

In 1906: 'A very successful concert was given in the Oddfellows Hall, Market Weighton, on Easter Monday, by the Town Prize Band, whose efforts on turning out on many occasions of public interest has made them very popular throughout the district, and consequently they should receive a fair share of engagements during the coming season. The concert was followed by a dance and everybody appeared to be having a real good time.'

In the same paper was the report:

'The Market Weighton choral society gave a concert in the Oddfellows Hall, Market Weighton, on Thursday evening. There was a large audience present who greatly enjoyed the entertainment.'

In 1910: 'The Market Weighton Pierrots reached high water mark at their latest concert held on Thursday week in the Oddfellows Hall. The latter was packed and several went away disappointed, neither standing or sitting room being available. £11 was raised to aid Hull Royal Infirmary. Great credit is due to the troupe managers, the staging effects etc. being splendidly carried out. The audience were not slow to show their appreciation of what beyond doubt was the best local entertainment provided in the town by purely local talent and amateurs. Encores were frequent.'

Market Weighton's first cinema, showing silent films, was there. Mr. Morley, who owned the building, started the cinema shows. When the Hornsey family lived in the house next door they continued showing films. The projector was housed in a fireproof cubicle and the audience sat on forms in front of the screen. The very

The Brass Band.

Market Weighton Wheelers Club, 1906.

small door into the Oddfellows Hall can still be seen. On entering you went up wooden stairs to the left which led into a room. To the left was the hall and to the right was a room where refreshments were served. The latter is still there, occupied by the Moore family.

Other activities included performances in aid of the East Yorkshire volunteers in 1915 and a football dance in aid of the newly formed football club in 1919,

Meetings were held to discuss the building of the Institute and, later, the church hall. Dances for the Market Weighton Wheelers Club's enthusiastic cyclists were also held there. In 1928 a whist drive was held in aid of the British Legion funds and the same week there was a St. Patrick's Carnival fancy dress parade. The report said:

'A CHARMING SCENE AT MARKET WEIGHTON
The Oddfellows Hall presented a pretty scene on St. Patrick's Eve, when the Recreation Committee of the Market Weighton St. Mary's Roman Catholic Church promoted a children's fancy costume parade.
The following took part:
Harold Bilton, (Chimney Sweep) Arthur Gawtrey, (Correspondence) Alfie Mizon, (Pierrot) George Hatfield, (Baker) Nora Hatfield, (Early Victorian) Rosie Turner, (King's Navy) Bessie Tennant, (Flower Girl) Norah King, (Marigold) Teddie Kneeshaw, (Woodbine Willie) Dorothy Hatfield, (Gibbs Dentifrice) Doreen Brown, (Rowntrees Chocolate) Mira Brown, (Fairy) Kathleen Kelsey, (Christmas Tree) Gladys Strangeway, (Oxo) Ivy Donkin, (Crestona Ginger Wine) Lillian Megginson, (Daffodil Fairy) Lilian Shaw, (Irish Boy) Marion Shaw, (Balloons) Dorothy Hird, (Peg Gypsy) Cissie Mizon, (Bat) Georgie Brown, (Cupid) Jennie Brown, (Punchinella) Madge Hudson, (Dick Whittington) Joan Hudson, (Gypsey Fortune Teller) Arthur Hudson, (Dutch) Jack Maynard, (Cowboy) John Maynard, (Pirate) Marie Carson, (Gypsey Dancer) Hermon Carson, (Iceberg) Matt Simmons, (St. Patrick Fairy) Dot Simmons, (Pierrette) Molly Baxter, (Courtier) George Gawtrey, (Boxer) Jessie Bond, (Hiawatha) Edna Bond, (Fairy in miniature) Alwyn Davis, (Pedlar) Dennis Hunter, (Dick Whittington) Audrey Saltmer and Marjorie Hunter, (Jack and Jill) Sheila Gauten, (Rowntrees Chocolate) John Goaten, (Oxo).'

Many of these children are remembered or are still alive, but, even more, the list of chosen costumes shows the children's interests of the day. There were no space men or television characters as would be today.

The same evening a dance was held which, the newspaper reported, –

'brought dancers from Houghton Hall, Nunburnholme, Londesborough, Shipton Thorpe, Holme on Spalding Moor and Market Weighton over which Councillor A. H. Sapcote presided as MC and excellent music was provided by the Market Weighton Syncopated Band.'

I understand that eventually they stopped having dances as the floor bounced so much that it was thought to be unsafe for dancing.

It was not an imposing building, having been built as a tannery, which is probably why I cannot find anybody who actually took a photograph of it from Finkle Street. It was very popular in the social life of Market Weighton until the church hall was opened, between Londesborough Road and Station Road, in 1933.

During the Second World War the Oddfellows Hall was used as a mess for the soldiers billeted in the town and, after the war, the last time I went in was to an auction sale of Miss Adams' furniture by Hornsey's Auctioneers. Brian Swann did his first selling when he sold the gardening tools in the small room, while Mr. Hornsey sold the furniture in the big hall. The main building was demolished and is now a car park and a garden planted by the Market Weighton Civic Trust.

THE CHURCH HALL 1933
The church magazine gave the following report:

'After an effort extending over eight years the new church hall has at last been erected. The building is 80 ft. long and 25 ft. wide and was opened by three representatives of the local Church of England Girls' Club in recognition of the work that that body had done to help the project . There is still a deficit on the building, about £250 being yet required. It is hoped to clear this off by the end of the year.'

In 1938 a smaller room was added and was used for meetings and Sunday School and later the play school. There was a kitchen, a stage and toilets at the other end of the main hall and an area outside

Mothers at a children's fancy dress.
Outside the Oddfellows Hall.

for parking cars. Once the Church Hall was opened it became the venue for most of the indoor activities of the town. Dances were regularly held and were usually attended by Mr. William Layton's dance band whose members often sat in basket chairs on the platform to perform. The local Amateur Dramatic Society gave very many excellent plays on the same stage and there were auction sales with furniture displayed both inside and out. The more expensive 'lots' were kept inside in case of rain. During the war it was sometimes used by Hymers College, Hull, junior school boys who were evacuated in Market Weighton whilst the senior boys were at Pocklington. As the boys had to share existing schools, any empty space was adapted as classrooms and for other uses, and the army, who were stationed in the town, would hold dances and concerts there.

The Church Hall.

My own memories cover many occasions, including my first proper dance during the war when we were invited to a concert by one of the officers in charge. Afterwards it was decided to move the chairs and have a dance and, as I was only 13, I had never been to a grown-up dance. A soldier asked me to dance and I was very shy. Later my sister asked me what he looked like, to which I replied, 'I don't know. I only saw his buttons.' Girls of 13 would not be so timid as that today.

My wedding reception and also that of my two daughters also took place in the hall. At our wedding the hall was in such a state after the war years that my father had it draped like a marquee to hide the dirty and shabby condition. Catering was by Mrs. Bastiman, who had a small café in the High Street.

In March 1973 at the Parish Church Council meeting the hourly rate of

The band that played in the Church Hall.

hiring the Church Hall was fixed as follows:

'Large Hall 80p., Small Hall 40p., Kitchen 30p. Parties, dances and similar events £10 for the occasion.'

In 1983 the church magazine reported that 'a few months ago the Church Hall was in a sorry state. The main door was falling off, with window frames bare and rotting, and the interior looked shabby and uninviting. Look at it now! It has been transformed by Bill Harrington and his working party – Alwyn Davis, Fred Saltmer and Laurie Lister. Thanks to their unstinting efforts and skill (not least in keeping down costs to an absolute minimum) we now have a building of which we can be proud. Thank you gentlemen.'

In March 1992, however, the Church Hall was bought by East Yorkshire Borough Council and it was decided that the cost of converting the old hall into a community hall would be substantial. The old hall was, therefore, demolished in July 1992 and work started on the new one in September. It was estimated that the new hall would cost £95,000, which was met by the Borough Council, and it is leased to the Market Weighton Town Council and managed by a committee. The hall has two rooms. One, larger than the other, has a polished dance floor and includes a movable stage. The smaller room is for meetings and the play group. A kitchen and toilets are included.

The Community Hall.

THE CINEMA

A large Georgian house stood where The Arch joins High Street opposite the building on Massey's Corner and next to the Red Lion public house. It was known as Bridge House and was at right angles to the street. At one time it was an inn called Board Inn, but, once closed as an inn, it was known as Bridge House. John Ramsdale was a dealer of spirits at the Board Inn, but in 1872 Mrs. Ramsdale was living at Bridge House, which must have been after the inn closed.

I have been told by Doreen Emmerson, who is Clifford Garforth's daughter, that, when the sun was in a certain direction, you could see the numbers on the bedroom doors, so it must have had rooms for visitors. It was called 'Bridge House' as in days gone by the beck, which flows from Springwells through Monkey Run and to the pond on The Green, went all the way

to the High Street above ground. Presumably there was a bridge near where the Georgian house stood. The beck was then diverted underground in a culvert and that little street was called The Arch. The beck now emerges again in the car park behind Netto and carries on along the edge of Scotts Croft. This is named after George Scott, or his descendants, who once owned the Oddfellows Hall and who owned that land and other property.

In 1927 Mr. Garforth bought Bridge House. At that time the deeds stated that the house was unoccupied. He built a hall attached to it called Central Hall. It is said that he wanted to build it over the culvert but was not allowed to, and because it was so close to the culvert extra strong foundations had to be put in to support it

In a November 1928 *Howdenshire Gazette* I found the following announcement:

'CONSERVATIVE GATHERING
Minister of Pensions at Market Weighton.
NO CLASS DISTINCTIONS
Individualism against Socialism
The Minister of Pensions, Major the Rt. Hon. G. C. Tryon, addressed a large public meeting in the New Central Hall, Market Weighton, on Saturday evening, when Major W.. H. Carver, M.P., for Howdenshire, presided.'

Major Carver said that, before starting the political part of the evening, he would like to congratulate the originator and erector of the new hall.

The Central Hall.

Bridge House on the left.

In the *Hull Times* of the same date was the following announcement:

'Speaking for the first time in the new Central Hall at Market Weighton on Saturday night, Major W. H. Carver M.P. complimented Mr. Garforth on the enterprise he had shown in building such a splendid hall and congratulated the people on having the use of it.'

There was a grand Carnival Ball in November 1928 to mark its opening. Mr. Garforth used the hall, not only for dances but to show silent films. I am told that the seats were movable and, when a dance or similar activity was taking place, they were stacked up away from the floor. Regulations then decreed that seats in cinemas must be fixed and so the Central Hall was extended with a large balcony and a new frontage and the floor was sloped with fixed seats. It then became Central Cinema. Mr. and Mrs. Garforth ran the cinema and, when I remember it, their son, Clifford, was the projectionist. On arriving at the cinema you had to queue to buy your ticket. Mr. Garforth would often welcome you in and I well remember him saying to me:

'You will enjoy this film, Miss Lyon. It's a very good film, Miss Lyon.'

On entering the foyer you bought your ticket from Mrs. Rosina Garforth, who stood at a double stable door which was open at the top and was the way into her kitchen. Later, I believe, a pay desk was made.

Each week two different films were shown, one Monday to Wednesday and another Thursday to Saturday, on which day there was a matinee. It was the main entertainment for many people, particularly courting couples. The cinema even had double seats at the back both downstairs and up on the balcony for their use. The stairs to the balcony were stone but to reach the seats you walked on bare wood. In those days many boys and men wore hob-nailed boots and as they walked up the bare boards they made a clatter, often after the film had started. At the front of the balcony was a low wall with , I believe, maroon velvet covering it – but maybe my memory deceives me.

The lights went out and we all thought the film would begin, but before that the screen was often filled with the numbers 10, 9, 8, 7, 6 and so on down to 0.

Central Cinema.

1947

This was accompanied by a chant of these numbers by many of the younger members of the audience. Now the film could start and, as I remember, as soon as this time came Clifford would emerge through the back doors of the pit with a ladder. He would walk down the aisle and prop the ladder up against the clock on the wall near the cinema screen. He then proceeded to wind it up, which then gave him time to return to the projection room before the next reel had to be switched on. This was very occasionally preceded by 10, 9, 8, and so on.

The boys would cheer and stamp their feet when the film became exciting, particularly when it was about cowboys and Indians. I have today been told of one occasion when a relation went to see a film at the cinema. In one scene where a man was creeping through a hall in the dark, a boy in the audience shouted out, 'Is your journey really necessary?'

One time I remember going to a film which was very popular and the cinema was full. The lights went out, followed by the usual procedure, and we all settled down to watch the film when a bright light from a large cinema torch was shone over the audience on the balcony and Mrs. Garforth shouted out:

'Has anyone kept a seat for Mr. Dixon?'

How many town cinemas, particularly today, would give that service? Whenever we had friends staying they were always taken to the Central Cinema as it was a great entertainment whatever the film was. My first date with my husband was to see a film called *'Caught in the Draft'* at the Central Cinema.

Sadly, when Mr. Garforth retired, it was sold to Mr. Prendagast who owned the Rialto and Clifton cinemas in York and, although Clifford was still the projectionist, somehow it was never quite the same again. When television came, the Central Cinema, Market Weighton, like so many more, closed and after some years was demolished and made into a car park, as was the old Georgian Bridge House which today would have been saved.

Immediately behind the cinema and looking out to the rear of the Oddfellows Hall was a very poor looking building known as the lodging house, where Irish men who came over to work on the farms lodged. I

Demolishing the lodging house.

remember its tiny windows. It too was demolished but this was not a great loss to the appearance of the town. All this is now car park.

Many houses and cottages down The Arch have been pulled down and this has altered the view as the backs of buildings on the High Street can be seen more easily. The Red Lion stands high and dry where once it was joined to other buildings.

If you stand with your back to Leake's butcher's shop on Southgate, the scene now is very different, as can be seen in the photographs. From the house

Early Southgate

Southgate looking north.

Southgate looking north, nearer High Street

Southgate looking north, Red Lion Inn in distance.

East side of Southgate, opposite Leake's butcher's shop

Southgate, looking towards Sancton Road.

Modern butcher's, Leake's on Southgate.

this was demolished and the Social Club built.

There have been many changes to the Market Hill, even within the last few years when the elegant bus shelter was built and the walled garden made. The photograph shows the houses which have been pulled down within living memory. The Alma Inn was in a prominent position but was demolished to widen York Road. The barber's and fish and chip shop which can be seen in the photograph of the view looking down the street when the Queen and Prince Philip came through, and the house next to the Alma Inn, which was used by Mr. Sutton, a dentist from Beverley, each week, have also gone.

At the back of the church was Mr. Copeland's fold yard, and beyond this the stack yard where now there are houses. Where the public toilets are situated was a brick building used to store the stalls ready for market day, when they were carried out into the narrow part of Market Place.

which has just been restored nearly to the far end on the east side of Southgate is now an industrial area instead of houses and cottages. On the west side two rows of cottages have gone and been replaced by modern houses and flats. The British Legion building used to be made of corrugated iron. It was built on a piece of land given by Colonel Langdale in 1929, but

The crowds waiting in Market Place to see the Royal car pass through.

On the left of Sancton Road, just beyond the bypass was a windmill. It was a construction of a type called 'tower mills', which were always made of brick walls inclined inwards. Most were painted with tar. It contained three floors, as was usual for that type of windmill. The higher floor contained bins for the grain. The middle floor which contained the mill stones was where the grinding took place. The ground floor comprised the meal floor, where flour was bagged up. It was demolished about 1970, I believe by the army as an exercise. The house is still there.

A building which had a comparatively short life was the Land Army Hostel. It was quickly built during the war, on the south corner of Londesborough Road and Goodmanham Road. It was built, eventually to house 70 girls who came from all walks of life to work on the farms to produce much needed food. There was a main wing which had in it the kitchen, common room, dining room and office and rooms for the warden. Behind this were the sleeping quarters forming the shape of a letter 'T'. At a later date to the rear, another wing was built for the same purpose. Each cubicle had a window and bunks to hold four girls, so they had little room to dress and must have spent most of their time in the common room. English films were shown some Saturday nights in the dining room and some of the girls sat on the tables at the back so that they could see. After the war the building was left empty but was later made into a petrol station by Robert B. Massey. Eventually it was demolished and the present bungalows built.

John Consitt Walker with Alice Smith outside the Alma Inn, about 1903.

The girls gardening behind the Land Army hostel.

The Land Army girls with Bob Speak, outside the hostel on Goodmanham Road.

The Alma Inn from Northgate looking towards Market Place.

HOW THE PEOPLE LIVED

Market Weighton, a market town in an agricultural area, would be expected to be the home of agricultural workers. The 1851 census shows that out of a population of 2,427 there were approximately 167 people working on farms living in the town. Many would of course, live outside the town on nearby farms. In spite of the population of the town declining to 2,290 in 1881, the number of agricultural workers had, against the normal trend for Yorkshire, risen to about 200. The population of the town continued to go down and in 1891 stood at 2,150. In 1999 it is up to 3,830 adults in Market Weighton on the electoral roll, with an estimate of about 3942 in 2000 .

There were other men working in agriculture. For example, about 30 farm servants, a pig jobber, shepherd, cattle dealer, agricultural band and twine makers and blacksmiths. According to the census, two shepherds were working away when the census was taken. This is understandable as it was always taken in March, the lambing season, when they could be living amongst the sheep. There were Irish casual workers, who usually lived in the lodging houses. Other men associated with agriculture were the mole catcher, who, in 1881, was called a vermin destroyer, game keeper, fell-monger, and carriers, who could have been for agriculture or other trades.

I looked at two years, 1851 and 1881, to discover in what type of work the people of the town were employed. The railway, having fairly recently arrived in 1851, we find that only six railway workers appeared to be living in Market Weighton: a railway clerk, two engine drivers, two railway guards and a labourer. No mention was made of a station master. In 1881 there were two clerks, four engine drivers, a fireman, two labourers, two plate-layers, five porters, a rullyman, a signal man, a station master, but now only one guard.

The gas works were in existence before 1851, and recorded in the census for that year was a gas manager and a stoker, but by 1881 there were also two men employed as gas fitters. Of other skilled craftsmen there were 23 joiners and carpenters but only five bricklayers, and apparently four painters.

Eddie Young, the cobbler, now retired.

It must remembered that jobs could be described differently between 1851 and 1881. Many of the wives went out to work but rarely declared this on the census. One said she was a maid of all work, two were mangle women, 15 were house servants, nine were housekeepers. It was interesting to note on looking at these two years of the census that there were no new houses being built, but then, as the population was on the decrease, they would not be needed. This is very different today with all the new housing estates being built in Market Weighton, but, of course, many people now live away from their place of employment, which was not possible earlier due to lack of transport.

At that time there were many occupations which would not be on a census today. How many of the following occupations will be recorded in Market Weighton in the year 2001:

Roper, band maker, shoe maker of whom there were 18, straw bonnet maker or even wheelwright, miller, tallow merchant, brewer's drayman, cordwainer, lace maker, stay maker, and cutlery and umbrella repairer?

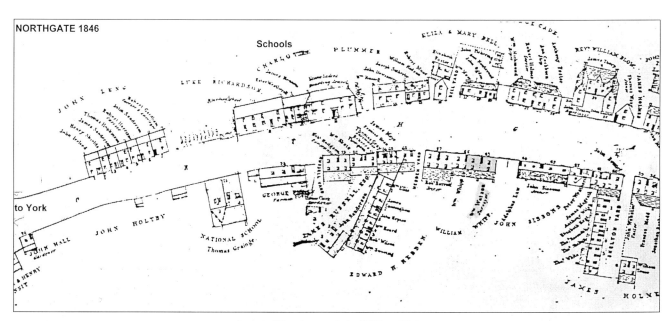

NORTHGATE 1846

A part of the plan made by William Watson

York Road cottages, now demolished.

Northgate, looking east. Railings removed during war.

Out of the 11 teachers shown in 1851, seven lived in Northgate. This was because, apart from the National School, built in 1841 at a cost of £700, which was on one side of the road, there were, on the other side, three schools or academies. Two were owned by a family called Richardson: the 'Gents' day and boarding school' run by the father, Luke Richardson, and a 'Young Ladies' day and boarding school' also carried on by his family. They all lived in the same house. There was another much smaller school nearer to the town. In the 1851 census Luke Richardson, schoolmaster, was 77 and married to Ann. His two daughters, Jane, aged 42, and Anne, aged 38, were both teachers and there was Francis, aged 31.

By 1881 Luke had died. I found he was buried at Barmby Moor, but the schools were now run by Anne, aged 68, Jane, 72, Mary, 56 and their brother William, 74. None of them married and obviously getting old so by this time there were no boarders. Many of these boarders in the past had come from farms outside Market Weighton as it would be difficult getting to a school.

In the old Methodist chapel seating plan it is interesting to see three pews for Mr. Richardson's boarders, Miss Richardson's boarders and Miss Plummer's boarders. These schools disappeared. One of the sites was not built on until 1999. Old cottages have been demolished, and a small new estate is going up. At one time the Richardson family appeared to have moved into Northgate House, which is now a residential home.

On Southgate there was a 'dame' school. The building survived until more recent years. Back in 1724 there was a free grammar school in Market Weighton of which Rev. T. Mitchell was the master. In 1842 the National School in Northgate was built for 200 pupils at a cost of £695. At the time there were 100 boys and 100 girls. In 1867 a building in Hungate, which had been a workhouse, was purchased from Mr. Musgrave by the church to be used for a girls' only school, whilst the one in Northgate would be for boys. The girls' school was officially opened in 1869 and in 1878 it was increased by one classroom.

In 1892 the Church Council were told by the Education Board that the playground at the girls' school must be enlarged because of the numbers of children at the school. Mr. Stephenson on behalf of the Church Council approached the Market Weighton Gas Light & Coke Company to see if the Church

Northgate House.

Boys' school, York Road.

Old girls' school, Hungate.

A much older Mr. Stephenson with more boys.

Market Weighton Boys' school with sports shield, 1930.
K. Playforth, W. Frankling, E. Swales,
? Brown, J. Wood, J. Smart, J. Maynard,
S. Hall, W. Crowther, H. Martin, E. Hall.
F. Hudson, R. Jackson, W. Edmunds,
G. Hatfield.

Girls at school 1921.

Council could buy an area, 10 feet by 27 feet for this purpose. Mr. Legge, the secretary, wrote back saying that no way would they sell but would let it to them on an initial two-year lease with a one-year lease thereafter. The annual rent was one shilling, starting in October 1892. They also paid 2s. 6d which was due for windows overlooking the Gas Company land. There were six small windows at the back of the original building prior to 1891 when two larger ones replaced two of them. In 1911 all six were increased in size.

The Education Board complained to the Market Weighton Church Council that, in the school building, there should be an area of 10 square feet per child. Mr. Stephenson wrote back saying that even on the basis of 10 square feet the school more than satisfied this requirement. There was an area of 1,109 square feet, the average attendance over the last five years being 93.3 children; 98.9 in 1905; 94.5 in 1906 and 93 in 1901 and the population of Market Weighton was not increasing. He said that the rooms were lofty and well lighted, the offices were conveniently placed, quite secluded and not opposite a window or door of the school. Having said that, it was decided in 1909 to change all the earth closets to water closets. As the Education Board thought the heating by 'Tortoise' stoves was insufficient to heat the classrooms, an open fire was put into each one and fire guards made available. It was thought that the teaching of infants

Boys at school 1921.

are 200 children taught in the Mount Pleasant Church of England School.

Market Weighton Infants School was opened by Lord Holderness in May 1980.

'Although we have been working hard in the new building since October we now officially exist,' said Rachel Mylne, the head mistress.

In 1898 the old Roman Catholic school was built and this also served as the Roman Catholic church until 1903 when a new church was built. Jerry Swales, who owned and ran the local horse-driven transport, took the children who attended there to school. He then took them home at the end of the day. They lived out in the farms some distance away. In the winter Mrs. Swales would bake potatoes in their jackets and, these, with a bit of salt, were given to each child to eat on the way home. This served two purposes. Firstly, it gave them something to eat at the end of the day and also kept their hands warm on the journey. Mr. Swales also owned the horse-

disturbed the older ones learning and so two large classrooms were divided, making four smaller ones. There were also complaints about the boys' school from the Education Board. In 1891 the boys' school had 140 names on the register. In 1899 the headmaster's house was extended in Northgate.

When the old school in Hungate closed in 1967, it was made into a private house. The boys' school in York Road also closed and was demolished except for the headmaster's house. All the children went to the new school built on Princess Road, and with the addition of three mobile classrooms had 12 years with 400 children in the one probably very overcrowded school. This can be contrasted with 1999 when there

Mr. Swales' wagonette, 1910, in Finkle Street.

St Mary's Hall.

drawn hearse, as did his father, John Wilson Swales, who had the wagonette seen in a photograph taken with many children riding in it at the coronation of George V in 1911.

Market Weighton School was originally called the County Secondary School. It was one of the first schools to be built after the Second World War by the East Riding of Yorkshire authority and according to a newspaper report cost £432 per place.

In September 1952 about 300 pupils attended the school. They came from Market Weighton, Holme on Spalding Moor, Newbald, Sancton, Shiptonthorpe, North and South Cliffe, Goodmanham, Bishop Burton, Middleton on the Wolds, Melbourne, Seaton Ross, Pocklington and Wilberfoss until schools were built at Pocklington

The old Roman Catholic Church and school.

Roman Catholic Church, 1998.

and Driffield. The Market Weighton school was officially opened in April 1953 and was locally known as 'The New School' for many years. At this time children took the 'eleven plus' exam at the junior school and, if they passed, the boys went to Beverley Grammar School and the girls to Beverley High School. All other children attended the County Secondary School at Market Weighton.

The school was well known for teaching agriculture as well as the traditional subjects. Many types of animal were cared for. The school adopted the six rowels (knight's spurs) which make up the school badge, and each represents one of the following: Sincerity, Honesty, Loyalty, Self-respect, Cleanliness and Industry. Lady Waechter de Grimston from Goodmanham was the first Chairperson of the Governors, and she presented the design to the school. It is now registered with the Royal Master at Arms, London. The wall plaque was a gift to the school, and bears testament to the years the Grimston family held office.

Neil Thwaites was the art teacher at the school from 1958 to 1992. He not only taught art but how to make corn dollies and also gave instruction to many other people in Market Weighton. He was known as the 'Corn Dolly Man'. He worked untiringly, making scenery for the dramatic productions and every year decorated the school hall for Christmas and helped in many other ways in the town and district. He was a founder member of the Guild of Straw Craftsmen and was national president, and revived the art of straw

dolly making. Neil died suddenly in February 1999. A book on Market Weighton could not be written without including such a talented person, one of those special characters so rarely found and loved by all today.

Away from the schools now, but back to Northgate. In the census we see mentioned two cow-keepers. One is still remembered by some people: Billy Bridge, whose family delivered milk in a can, measuring it out into the customer's jug with a measure on a long handle. They continued until regulations prevented it or they became too old to carry on. There was Tommy, Billy's son, and Billy's sister, Milly, who I remember walking right up Londesborough Road carrying her heavy can for just one loyal customer. She had carried the can so much that her back was twisted over and she walked like that whether the can was in her hand or not. I remember she was always dressed in black and wore a funny little black hat.

Looking through old newspapers I found in 1895 the following report about the Bridge family:

'On Monday night, a son of Mr. Bridge of Market Weighton went into a field near Red House, with the purpose of bringing away a calf. He got the calf into the trap when the horse began to kick and eventually ran into the next field, where it

The milkman delivering milk in 1997 on Cliffe Road.

Neil Thwaites, the Corn Dolly man, in High Street, '50 years on VE Day'.

Billy Bridge with milk.

dropped dead. The loss will be a serious one to the owner as he had sold the horse which was to be delivered the next day. It was not insured.'

As we are still in Northgate it would be appropriate to mention two more characters who lived in that same street. Keith Lowe has already written about the first one very recently. He is William Bradley, who had a house built at the very beginning of Northgate which has survived, having been owned for many years by the France family. William is known as Giant Bradley and in recent years the town has remembered him each May on 'Giant Bradley day'. He was born here in February 1787 to John, a tailor, and Ann Bradley and was one of a large family. William weighed 14 pounds at birth. By the time he was 20 he weighed 27 stone and was 7 feet 9 inches tall. He is still recorded in the *Guinness Book of Records* as the tallest person in Great Britain. After about ten years exhibiting himself all over the country he retired, unwell, to his home town and had a house specially built in Northgate. This house was built on the site of the house where he was born but was made with the rooms high enough for him not to feel cramped. Unfortunately he became lame and also developed tuberculosis and died at the age of 33 and was buried in the churchyard at Market Weighton church. At the west end of the inside wall of the church is a memorial to him:

In Memory of
WILLIAM BRADLEY
Son of John and Ann Bradley
Who died May 30th 1820
aged 33
He measured
Seven feet nine inches in height
and Weighed
twenty seven stones

The second man, whilst not generally so famous, has given to the people of Market Weighton an asset rarely available to even much more important towns. This is William Watson, a land surveyor who lived in Northgate many years ago. He drew the detailed plan of Market Weighton in 1848 and did the same for Pocklington later. He also drew a plan of the seating in the three independent chapels of Market Weighton, including the Wesleyan, Primitive and Independent chapels in 1849, showing who used each pew

Giant Bradley Day. Line dancing in High Street.

Christopher Greener, the present-day tallest man, who comes on Giant Bradley day.

Giant Bradley's house.

by payment to the chapel authorities. His address when he drew this was given as 65 Northgate, Market Weighton.

William Watson was born in May 1784, the son of a Seaton Ross farmer, John Watson and his wife Sarah. They were both from farming stock. William Watson himself carried on the family tradition at Seaton Lodge or Common Farm. He was responsible for ridding the land of heath and furze until by 1834 it had become productive farm land. He farmed there until 1838, but he was also a surveyor and maker of sundials. The farm became known as Dial Farm because of the number of sundials he erected on it. The wonderfully detailed maps of Market Weighton and Pocklington were not drawn until he was older and while he was living at different times in these two towns. Five of his brothers farmed in the area, one at Thorpe le Street, another at Holme on Spalding Moor and two in Seaton Ross. Only the eldest brother left the area and emigrated to America.

The Market Weighton plan, drawn at a scale of 21 yards to the inch, was available in both a plain edition at five shillings and a coloured version at six shillings. A copy hangs in All Saints church today, and one in the Londesborough Arms. The plan is unique because not only does it show each building in elevation but indicates which have thatched roofs and which also are outbuildings. It shows the tenant's name for each property and in many cases the occupation and then the owner in capital letters. The maps were sold by William Boast, a local bookseller. In 1855 William Watson produced a similar map of Pocklington only two years before he died unmarried in Seaton Ross in December 1857, and was buried with the rest of his family in the churchyard there. The value of these maps is probably far more appreciated now than when they were drawn as they provide a very vivid insight into what Market Weighton was like in the mid-19th century.

Another man living in Northgate at that time could have been Market Weighton's first attorney. John Seaton West Kirkpatrick was born in Gilberdyke in about 1823 and at 25 he was living in Northgate, Market Weighton. He then moved to a house on the High Street, but by 1872 he had a house built on Londesborough Road which he called The Aspens. When he died, some time after 1901, his sister continued to live there until after 1911. She and her next-door neighbour, John Proudlock, did not agree and so she built the very high wall between the two properties which is still there today. Her house was then bought by Dr. R. H. Ashwin and its name changed

The Aspens, later Waldyve House

to Waldyve House. Opposite were aspen trees which survived until a gale blew one on to the new surgery car park. At the far end of the garden facing York Road two cottages were built for the groom and another servant.

Inside the old surgery waiting room.

The way into the old surgery. With the night speaking tube.

Londesborough Road.

New surgery, built 1964, but with many later extensions.

Ashfield House, on Londesborough Road.

Dr. Ashwin had the surgery at the side of his house. It is incredible to think that such a small building was big enough to be used by two doctors and serve the medical needs of the town, but it did. The surgery today, across the road, is very different and gets bigger as time goes by. On the door of the old surgery is the night speaking-tube. A bell was rung into Dr. Ashwin's bedroom and the messenger spoke into a metal tube to the doctor's bedroom. There was also a bell to use in the daytime. The surgery contained a waiting room with a high-backed wooden settle and there were two steps up to each surgery. One of these was also the dispensary. A door led into the doctor's house. My children were always tempted by the steps and I had great difficulty in stopping them jumping down from them. When Dr. Ashwin retired Dr. R. P. Butler carried on along with his son, Dr. R. M. Butler and other doctors and they were responsible for building the new surgery. There were no nurses working in the old surgery, nor was there a receptionist. It is also strange to say that Dr. Ashwin operated to remove my tonsils with Dr. R. P. Butler as the anaesthetist in 1937. The operation was conducted on a table in my own bedroom.

Ashfield House, further up Londesborough Road, was built around the middle of the 19th century and was occupied soon after that by the local practitioner, Dr. Matthew Jackson, who in 1848 lived in the High Street where Barclays Bank is now. A window in the church is dedicated to him. Following Dr. Jackson at Ashfield was Dr. A. G. R. Harris, the medical officer for District Two. It was then bought by the Simpson's, who owned the Brewery and the Londesborough Arms. When Mr. Simpson died his two daughters, Annie and Ida, resided there but later found it too big and it was sold to George Newbury, my uncle, a butcher in High Street, in 1928. A person who was a servant for the Simpson family remembered seeing the coachman bring round the coach and horses and the family, grandly attired, being taken to balls at Londesborough Hall.

The Wicstun Veterinary Group was started by Mr. R. J. Hickes in Scott Yard and then Mr. J. P. Cook moved it to Londesborough Road. The practice later went into the present property, originally a private house once owned by the Farmer family. The veterinary service has expanded and now has surgeries at Pocklington and South Cave. A much enlarged practice, it is now called Wicstun Veterinary Group.

Dentists used to come from Beverley once a week and have their surgeries in the front rooms of private houses. It was a Beverley dentist who started a permanent surgery upstairs in the chemist's premises until the new one was made in the yard, as described in another part of the book.

On Beverley Road, now the factory for Burgess's ice-cream, Mr. W. Hipwell built a factory which was supposed to represent cottage industry. It was called Daneswear and employed people from Market Weighton and district for many years. When he retired the factory was bought by Allard Knitwear and remained so until it was bought by Burgess of Beverley

Wicstun Veterinary Group and Social Club.

making ice-cream. The buildings have, over the years, been increased, but the original Daneswear building is still there.

The firm of Robert B. Massey and its subsidiaries have been the main employers for Market Weighton people from just after the war until his retirement. All the industrial property on the left of Southgate once belonged to this firm, now Europower and others, as were the factory and agricultural store on Holme Road and the main garage and workshops which were on the corner of High Street and Southgate. Mrs. Massey gave the land and club house for the Market Weighton Bowls Club after the death of her husband, who also owned and farmed Wold House Farm on Beverley Road.

Mr. Hipwell's factory, Beverley Road, now Burgess's

The firm of J. Dawson and Sons on Londesborough Road has been associated with Market Weighton for many years. The site was bought after the war from the Air Ministry, who had commandeered it at the beginning of the war for repair works. One of the original buildings is still in use. Dawson's are corn and seed merchants and corn dryers, and around harvest time employ many students as well as regular local employees. The firm started in the Leeds area. They owned farms in the East Riding for many years. The business is still owned by the family. Before acquiring a property in Market Weighton they attended the corn market each week at the Londesborough Arms.

The Bowling Club on Beverley Road.

A building on Holme Road which looks very much like a public hall but has never been used for this purpose is the one which recently belonged to R. Yates & Son which sells agricultural supplies. This was built by Mr. Cockburn as a knitting factory. In 1914, a newspaper article stated:

'500 PAIRS OF WOOLLEN SOCKS will be knitted free of charge for our soldiers. As proprietor of the Diamond Hosiery Company, hosiery manufacturers, Market Weighton, I will gladly knit the above quantity of socks for anyone in the East Riding who wishes to forward any particular quantity of wool. I shall be pleased to make from 1 to 12 pairs for any one person. I have suitable machinery for any class or thickness of wool, so you can scarcely get wrong whatever you forward me in the way of wool. I also undertake to return the goods very promptly.'

Collison's staff 1944-1945.
Bob Foster, Jimmy Beales, Doris Wright, Norma Blakestone, Sam Flintoft, Dick Smith, ? Sanderson, William Bradley.

Ethel Malyon née Potter says that her mother worked there and Mr. Cockburn used to say:

'We won't have any drones in this busy bee hive.'

Just before the war Collison's Agricultural Machinery company bought the premises from Cockburn's and Mr. Collison's daughter, Doris, looked after it.

Collison's billhead 1953.

Telephones
BEVERLEY 400 (2 LINES)
MARKET WEIGHTON 104
DRIFFIELD 113

COLLISONS
(BEVERLEY) LIMITED.

Depots
HULL
MARKET WEIGHTON
DRIFFIELD

NORWOOD, BEVERLEY

AGRICULTURAL AND MOTOR ENGINEERS
IMPLEMENT MAKERS AND AGENTS

When the war started in September 1939, the army commandeered the field at the side for parking army tanks and also the upstairs of the building as a soldiers' mess.

As they had taken away the kitchen where Doris used to prepare her dinner, the army cook supplied it to her every day, while she was running the agricultural sales downstairs. They allowed Collison's to carry on business because of the connection with food for the nation.

When Doris was to be married in Beverley Minster it was deep snow and she was taken to Beverley in an army vehicle. The soldiers said they would take their band over to Beverley at night to play for a dance but they only got as far as Deep Dale and could get no further. Doris and her husband, Harry Wright, who was on embarkation leave, were going to Chester for their honeymoon but there were no trains, again because of the snow. This was January 1941. The regiments which at that time were stationed at Market Weighton were the 3rd and 4th Hussars and the RASC, who maintained the tanks in Collison's field. Yates of Malton bought the building and business. David Manson, who was manager, later bought it and at present it is called MW Farm Supplies and still sells to farmers, which means that it has been 60 years in the same trade.

York Road is now the area of a small industrial estate. The location chosen is situated just before the old route of the Selby line of the railway. There was a bridge over the road just beyond this estate which was demolished when the railway lines had been removed.

At the bottom of Beverley Road were two houses which were demolished to widen the road. One belonged to Harrison's who owned threshing machines. There were also traction engines stored in the yard at the Oddfellows Hall.

Hannah Jewison owned land behind the Londesborough Arms in 1848 and on this land Robert

The railway bridge on York Road.

and John Jewison built and owned a large brewery. It was built in 1875 and the architect was William Hawe. Its vast size and height dwarfed the buildings around it. It had a capacity of ten quarters and a large ale and spirit store. This property was sold to Simpson and Co. about 1867. Richard Simpson, who lived at Ashfield, was the main partner. The Simpson family were also at the Londesborough Arms. Eleven men were employed at the brewery in 1881. The census of that year shows a brewer, brewer's clerk, brewer's drayman, maltster and labourers. The brewery was sold in 1899 to John Smith's Tadcaster Brewery, which used it as a maltings until 1935. In 1985 there was a very destructive fire which destroyed a part of it when it was being used as small industrial units. Left empty for some time, it was eventually demolished in 1989 and in its place was built a £2 million block of about 48 flats for the elderly to a similar size and shape as the old building. The complex was called All Saints Court and opened in 1991.

This particular year was important for Market Weighton. The bypass was constructed and opened, the Londesborough Arms re-opened after extensive alterations, the new community hall was opened and the first turf was laid for the new bowling green by Mrs. Muriel Massey. Confidence in the future of the town is growing, more houses being built and the population increasing, as it is at the beginning of the 21st century.

Showing the brewery after the fire. Taken from The Arch.

All Saints Court. The flats were built after the brewery was demolished.

A SHOP ON MARKET PLACE

In the street called Market Place, previously known as Highgate, in the centre of Market Weighton, is a property which holds many memories for me and many members of my family. It is not an important building and has no great architectural features but, like all old buildings, holds some history and I'm sure many secrets. My family have had connections with the premises in Market Place since before 1800 and the Lyon family owned it almost right through until my father retired in 1959. It was when my husband, Tom, and I became interested in family history that natural progression led us to wonder about the history of this very ordinary but interesting part of my family history.

The first mention of a transaction was when a gentleman by the name of John Barker, a yeoman, who lived at Sutton on Derwent, sold it to his two sons, John and Robert Barker, in February 1714. Robert Barker, a grocer, and his wife, Catherine, lived there and had, among others, two daughters, Eleanor and Dorothy. Robert Barker died and left the home to his daughters. His wife continued to live there with them. There are several memorials to this family on the walls of All Saints church. Catherine and her daughter, Eleanor, died leaving the only surviving sister, Dorothy. In the meantime, at a date prior to 1801, John Lyon, a weaver from Sancton, occupied the house as a tenant, as did Robert Roantree. We know that John Lyon had married Ann Moor, whose father was also a weaver in Market Weighton, although Ann was born in Newbald. Possibly John had been an apprentice with Joseph Moor. The same

Moor family still live in Market Weighton at the turn of the 20th century.

In 1801 Dorothy Barker died and in her will left £600 for the distribution of four-penny loaves every fortnight, 30 among the poor of Market Weighton and ten among those of Shipton, and directed the surplus income to be distributed among the poor of the two townships at the discretion of the vicar and church wardens at Easter and Christmas. Her premises on the south side of Market Place were to be sold. John Lyon, a weaver, with the help of his brother. Thomas Lyon, a carpenter, living and working in Newbald, decided to buy the premises and safeguard John's home. The sale went through on 'the eleventh day of September 1801'. The deeds of this sale described it as 'a messuage or tenement with the dovecote, yard, garth, close and rating pit on the backside thereof'. (A 'rating pit' can be called a 'retting pit' and is a pit of water in which is laid flax to 'ret' or rot in readiness for weaving or rope making.)

Previously, in 1715, so the story passed down through the generations recalls, two young men from the Glamis area were in trouble or danger connected with the Stuart cause. They escaped to England carrying a letter from Lord Lovatt to Lord Langdale, asking him to take them in and help them. This he did, and, although William Lyon seems to have moved away, the one fact we know is that John Lyon married, and his family lived in the Sancton area. His son, Thomas, a yeoman, married Jane Huard in 1753. They lived and had land in Sancton and had five children. The eldest one was again called John. It was he who,

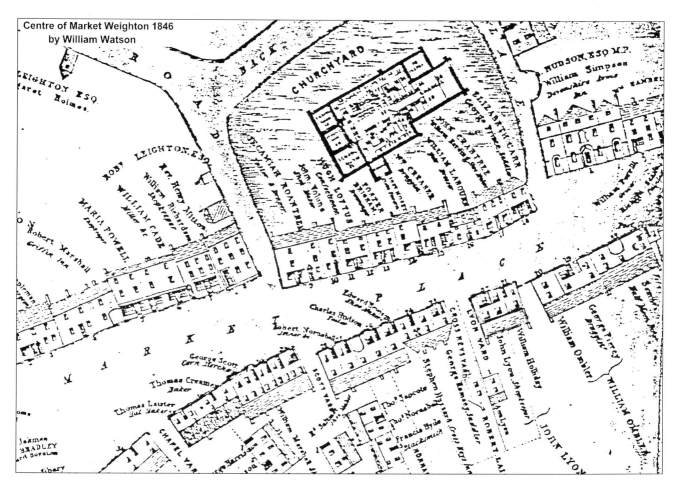

Centre of Market Weighton 1846 by William Watson

Jane, wife of John Lyon, 1793-1860.

Sancton churchyard.

in 1801, had purchased the shop premises at Market Weighton, and at the same time a close of land of five acres which Eleanor Barker had acquired at the time of the enclosures. This land was situated at Sandfield on the Holme Road in Market Weighton. What really surprised us was that, just one day later, John Lyon mortgaged all this to William Carr, a yeoman of Sancton. William Carr held the property in Market Place until he died and then John Lyon obtained it back from the trustees in October 1810. He did not, however, appear to take back the five acres on Holme Road. For the next eight years he owned the premises outright and during that time built a cottage and a small warehouse adjoining on part of the yard. This cottage lay on the west side of the yard. He mortgaged it again for various periods of time.

In 1821 John and Ann Lyon's eldest son, another John, who was born in Market Place, Market Weighton, married Jane Holliday, a spinster from Gowthorpe, at Pocklington church. He was described as 'Grocer' in the church records when their first child, Elizabeth, was baptised. When William and Ann were christened he was a 'Grocer and twine spinner'. This was in 1828 and 1830. He was also a rope maker; in the buildings on the east side of the yard near the bottom is the area which was the rope walk. My father has told me which one it was, but unfortunately I have forgotten. John and Jane are also shown there in 1848 on the plan of Market Weighton, with Jane's father, William Holliday, living in the house adjoining on the street side. He was a retired officer of excise and the Excise Office was in the Old Kings Arms in High Street.

Ann Lyon, John the weaver's widow was living in the cottage built by her husband on the west side of the yard. John had died in 1837 aged 78 and we think was buried in Sancton churchyard. His wife, Ann, lived to 91 and was looked after by her unmarried daughter, Mary.

In 1860 John junior's wife, Jane, died, and he married Elizabeth Braithwaite,

a widow from Shipton. In 1861 John died there. He left the shop premises to his son, William, but the cottage in the yard, where his mother had lived, was left to his new wife, Elizabeth, for her life. John and Jane were buried in Sancton churchyard, with a memorial stone which has now been eroded but was fortunately photographed by us while it was still readable and recorded by the East Yorkshire Family History Society. Nearby is a very old gravestone where Jane Lyon née Huard was buried in 1784 and also their daughter-in-law, Charlotte, the wife of Thomas Lyon of Newbald, whose maiden name was Appleton.

William, as we saw in the 1851 census, trained as a grocer and was later also a seedsman and farmer. The buildings at the bottom end of the yard were farm buildings at this time. In August 1858 William was married to Mary Green from Goodmanham Lodge at

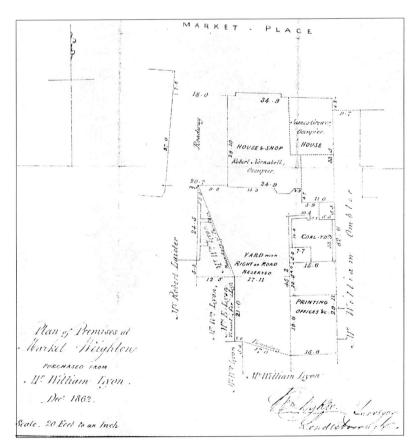

31

Market Weighton church by Rev. Joseph Foxley.

In January 1863 William sold the front part of the premises to George Hesp of Settrington, a farmer, and Henry Jackson of New Malton, a gentleman. This included the property on the south side of the Market Place, a printing works and the yard around it. This left William with the following property: 'dwelling house, cottage, yard, warehouse, barn, granary, loose box, stable, root house, pigsties, fold yard, cart shed, steaming house, gig house, privies, ash pit and garden situated on the south side'.

From 1863 to 1872 William was a grocer, draper and a farmer and seeds man and had a right of way from the front street:

'of nine feet in width measuring from the said messuage or dwelling house now in the occupation of Robert Nornabell to the corner of the wall dividing the said premises from the premises adjoining on the west and of sufficient width along the said yard for horses, cattle, carts and carriages at all times herewith for the said William Lyon his heirs and assigns to pass and repass along and across so much of the said yard as is hereby granted'.

William Lyon also had to be given access to and be allowed to use the pump situated behind the house occupied by Robert Nornabell. When Elizabeth Lyon, William's stepmother, died, his aunt, Jane Galland occupied the cottage. She had previously lived in Newbald and her tombstone can be seen in the churchyard there; its memorial also mentions her husband George. It seems that during that time William built or adapted two or possibly three more cottages. As in 1872 there were other people living in the yard. The indenture mentions the following people: William Lyon, Mrs. Anne Wilson (who could be one of his wife's relations), Mrs. Jane Galland (his aunt, and sister to John Lyon, rope maker and grocer), William Harding and Francis Brown. In 1872 William Lyon must have had a desire for adventure and the wide open spaces because he mortgaged the rest of his property to George Hesp and, buying saddles and other harness, sailed for America with his young family.

Thomas, who was my grandfather, was about 12 and remembered when they landed in America seeing the wooden sidewalks or footpaths burning fiercely in the town to which they came, It was a great fire and killed many people. It was not surprising that the sidewalks burned as they were made of resinous pine wood like the roof of the only pumping station supplying water for fighting the fire, and nearly all the houses.

None of us know why, after possibly only months, they sailed back home. Nobody ever told us what went wrong. Maybe they wanted to forget. It could have been poor health as two children died just after they returned. The next

evidence we have of their return is a bill headed:

'William Lyon 1873 – Family grocer, tea dealer, Italian Warehouseman and Provision Merchant, – selling glass, china and Staffordshire ware.'

This was found many years later by a builder pulling

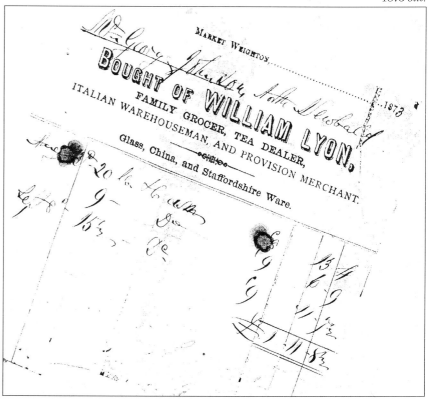

1867 Lyon advert.

1873 bill.

William Lyon, 1830-1874.

Mary, wife of William Lyon, 1838-1925.

down a wall of a cottage in Newbald and was given to William Lyon's grandson, my father, Harold William Lyon.

William must have still wanted to farm because he bought about ten acres of land called Northfields on the Londesborough Road, which he had rented before he went to America. The deeds were exchanged but William died of gastric fever and peritonitis in 1874 and so it was immediately resold and signed by one of his trustees, his brother-in-law, Thomas Green of Goodmanham Lodge.

The tragedy of the American episode and the loss of a husband was bad enough but that was not all. Two of their little children had died and were buried in their father's grave in the graveyard on

China. George, Ida, Gladys and Wilfred Miles.

Londesborough Road, not very far from the field he was about to buy when he died. Mary Lyon must have been a very brave and determined lady as she ran the business with the help of her young son, Thomas, who was only 16. Later her second son, Francis, also assisted in the shop. He eventually ran a grocery business at Leyburn. It is amazing that in 1888 when Ida, one of her daughters, was 18 she was allowed to go out to China as a teacher of English in a girls' school in Hankow. While there she married a missionary, George Miles, and was taken to what was described as 'a heathen city', where she was the first Christian woman to live. They had four children who quite often had to be lowered from the windows at the back of the home to avoid riots at the front. When they wanted educating they were sent back to England and stayed during holidays at the shop house with their 'Uncle Thomas and Aunt Maggie'. It is amazing at that time that she was allowed to go, particularly a girl of that age, and when her mother was a widow. Ida and George Miles were the grandparents of Bruce and Elaine Miles and their sister Beatrice, and Wilfred Miles was one of the children born out there.

Mary Lyon got back the front part of the property from George Hesp and it seems that from that day the business went from strength to strength. A calendar given by her to the customers in 1877 is still in my possession. Thomas, her eldest son, married Mary Jane Kelsey, who was a local girl and daughter

Looking up the shop yard. Early photograph.

Letter to customers when the business was transferred from Mary to Thomas G. Lyon, 1890.

of Gideon Kelsey, a shoemaker. They moved into the shop house and his mother moved into the cottage in the yard. Eventually she went to live in a house in Westfield Terrace off Holme Road, where she stayed until she died in 1925. Thomas lost his wife after she had given birth to their fourth child, who also died. He was left with three little daughters. He did eventually marry his cousin, Margaret Green from Goodmanham Lodge, and they had two children, Harold William and Hilda Margaret.

In September 1890 Mary handed over the business to Thomas, who had managed it for 14 years. The letter sent to customers is shown in this book. The language is formal and flowery compared with today's. In 1891 and 1892 all the property at the shop in Market Place was bought from her by Thomas Lyon, which brought it all back into one ownership. In about 1898 he did a major alteration to the property facing the street by adding a third storey. This was to accommodate apprentices and later a printing room. There were also extensions made to the warehouses.

A newspaper cutting in 1909 gave the following information:

'WORKMEN ENTERTAINED – A very successful and enjoyable time was spent on Thursday, January 14th when Mr. T. G. Lyon, grocer of the Central Stores, Market Weighton, entertained the workmen employed at the store and their friends numbering 60, to a very sumptuous tea and supper in the Wesleyan schoolroom. Games of a great variety was provided and the harmony of the evening was contributed to by Miss Dorothy Stephenson and Miss Hilda Lyon (pianoforte solos), Miss Elsie Lyon, Mr. W. P. Wilson and Mr. S. H. Cooper (songs), and some excellent selections on the gramophone were given by Mr. P. Beal, whilst a sketch given by Mr. Wilson was highly appreciated by the audience. Mr. A. Johnson proposed "Success to the firm" and thanked Mr. Lyon for his kindness in entertaining them so handsomely. This was

Advert, Thomas. G. Lyon, 1892.

Thomas G. Lyon, J.P., 1859-1946

Shop front, 1900.

A letter tothe customers.

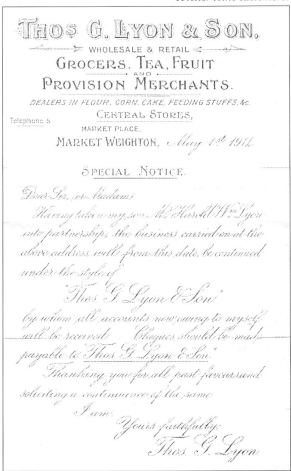

Advert, 1905

*The back of Thomas G. Lyon's shop, 1921,
showing the early lean-to office.*

seconded by Mr. T. Hebden and carried with acclamation. This terminated a very merry evening for the workmen.'

This could have been an annual event as there were other reports in other newspapers.

At Christmas 1909 Thomas's only son, Harold William, my father, left school. He started work in the shop the next day. He worked in all the departments and at every job to give him a thorough training. In May 1914 he was taken into partnership with his father and the name was changed from 'Thomas G. Lyon' to 'Thomas. G. Lyon and Son'. Only four months later my father was called up with the East Riding Yeomanry as the First World War had begun. He spent over four years out in Egypt and Palestine. Meantime life had to go on in the Market Place and my grandfather was helped by his daughter, Annie, who worked in the office. At the end of the war in 1919 my father was demobilised and came home and married. Two years later he took over the business when my grandfather retired.

Thomas had worked hard and built up the business. The service was not just available to the people of Market Weighton. Travellers went round the countryside finding out what the housewife would need in the next fortnight. They travelled on horseback and later on motorcycles, but in about 1928

Shop yard, 1912.

they were given the added luxury of motor cars. The orders were collected together in a room known as 'The Back Shop' and put into wooden boxes. The sugar, flour and other dry ingredients were weighed up in paper bags, sugar always being in blue bags. The lard, butter and margarine were cut into blocks according to the weight required, and wrapped in greaseproof paper. Vinegar and paraffin were put into earthenware jugs, and treacle and golden syrup run out of the big barrels into stone jars. All these were marked with the name of the business. Some still exist today.

The boxes containing the groceries were carefully stacked on to, firstly, carts pulled by horses, and, later, lorries. The drivers delivered the goods and took away the empty bottles and stone jars and jugs. In winter, conditions were often very difficult as many of the customers lived on remote farms and the snow could be deep on the Wolds above Market Weighton. During this sort of weather sledges were taken on the lorries and were often pulled across fields in order to make sure that the farmer's wife was not without food. Animal foods were also delivered along with the groceries. Locally, small quantities of goods were delivered by an errand boy who went round on a bicycle with a large basket on the front, but the bigger orders were delivered every week. This was the service which was expected in those days and was continued as long as the business was run by my family.

Cutting lard, 1957.

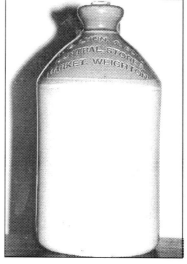

Vinegar bottle from Thomas G. Lyon & Son.

Bagging sugar, in the back shop, 1957.

Blue Cross.

Shop front, 1924.

Harold W. Lyon, J.P., 1893-1967.

An article written about the shops in Market Weighton in 1926/27 describes the equipment in the shop:

'Market Weighton has some up-to-date shops. One which deals chiefly in foodstuffs is remarkable for the efficient methods and modern plant employed. Some of the appliances installed are – Electric lighting throughout premises, Berkel slicing machine, Universal electric coffee mill, Five 'True Weight' Automatic scales, Gardner Baking Powder Sifter and Mixer, Duckworth Double-conical Fruit Cleaning Machine, Lister butter and Margarine Moulding Machine, Bentall Combined Corn Rolling, Grinding and Screening Mill, 11 hp Hornsby Oil Engine, 3 hp Amanco Oil Engine, Kobler Electric Lighting Plant (Automatic), 110 volts, 2,000 watts, 'Marksway' Patent Lard Cutting Machine, Gestetner Rotary Duplicator, Royal No 10 Typewriter, Masseeley Ticket and Showcard Printing Machine and Outfit, Elliot Addressamite Addressing Machine with stencil for each customer and most of their wholesale firms and travellers, Adana Printing Machine, Kardex Card Indexing System, Pratts Petrol Pump and underground storage, Burroughs Adding Machine, Delivery by horse, One ton Ford and three ton Daimler, three Douglas motor cycles for travellers. Evidently a shop that is fitted for service. Messrs. T. G. Lyon & Son are to be congratulated upon their business enterprise.'

In 1926 the premises were wired up for electricity, and just finished before the general strike. The generators not only gave the shop and house the benefit of lighting but, according to an article in December 1932 in *Town and Country News*:

'The whole premises are lighted by a generating plant which also supplies power for refrigeration of a cold room of 500 cubic feet capacity, this being used for the storage of bacon and other provisions which are likely to deterioration.'

Just through the front gate was the petrol pump, installed for the cars and lorries which in those days

Shop yard, 1928.

were not run on diesel. Behind this were the buildings on the right. Upstairs was an office, and, underneath it, a refrigerated bacon room and a cheese room in which were slatted shelves where full-sized farmhouse cheeses were stored and turned regularly.

I was given a postcard headed, 'THE ENTER-PRISE VAN', dated 1930. I was very interested as I was too young to remember it, although my sisters did. I went to visit Allan Johnson, who had worked for my father at that time. He was then 91. I took a tape recording and the following is what he told me about the van. It was bought in 1930 to act as a

AT YOUR SERVICE

THOS. G. LYON & SON, Central Stores, Market Weighton. Telephone No. 5.

Early Lyon van.

travelling shop and postcards showing the van were sent out to the customers:

'It was a bit secret. It came from London. Your father and Harold Martin went to fetch it. We were not supposed to know about it but, once someone knows anything, it can't be a secret any more.

At the top of the van there were ventilators and when it rained the water went on to the shelves so extra louvres were put on.

When it went up to Goodmanham it couldn't get up the hill and the two-ton Daimler had to pull it up. That was a lovely lorry and lasted a long time. He put too much in it (the van). Well, you know, he wanted to supply all East Yorkshire with it. The shelves were very wide and were at both sides of the van and sloped to stop things falling off when it went round a corner. There was a counter. It wasn't a self-service. When you got the shelves filled there was a lot of weight. When you think how heavy even the shopping

you collect in a basket is you can imagine what weight it had to carry. You said what you wanted and the man got it for you.'

I asked him how long my father used it but he said it was such a long time ago he couldn't remember.

'I shouldn't think it was there for more than a year,' he said.

I said it obviously was a failure, to which he replied,

'Shall we say – it wasn't a success. The engine was not big enough. The size of the wheels was not big enough for the big vehicle and the country roads.' He then continued, 'I don't know what happened. I think Percy Beal had been to London and he said he saw The Enterprise. If Tom Hebden heard anything he went straight up to the office, so Percy Beal was sent for into the office. We decided that someone had bought it and not paid for it and that was the annoying part about it and, if he had seen it, that was wrong. You know you can think what you like, can't you? Motor dealing was like horse dealing. We wondered, and it made the experience much worse. Somebody must have been running it around in London. I don't know, but, of course, in those days I wasn't in a position to know what was going on like I was later. I knew everything then... Balloons were sent off but I don't know how many. It said on them to look out for a surprise and then it got to "A surprise in store" and then the cards went. I don't think they went by post but I think they would be taken out with the order. I haven't much recollection of the cards.'

The old shop in 1932.

The bacon counter in the new shop, 1934.

Shop coffee grinder, 1934.

Shop interior, 1934.

Shop window dressing.

Shop front, 1957.

Shop window dressing, 1957.

(Allan Johnson died in February 1998 aged 92. He started working at the shop in 1922.)

In 1932 my father decided to move house and extend the shop the full width of the building. Our new house, which he had built by Tarran's of Hull, with the architect Blackmore and Sykes, was on Londesborough Road on land belonging to Mr. Copeland. It was called Tel-el-Fara after a hill in Palestine. As soon as we moved out the builders moved into the shop house. My memories of that time are of the excitement of a new home and I have very few recollections of the huge changes that were taking place in Market Place.

The new shop was considered very modern, but the service was just the same as before. Chairs were provided to allow customers to rest, and the smell of coffee being ground always brings in the customers. Several people today still remark about this. In the windows and the shop were large displays of packets and tinned goods which were changed each week. I remember Walter Playforth doing this very artistically. Large tins of biscuits were lined up along one side of the shop and each had a glass lid so that the customer could decide which variety would be purchased. Above this were display cases with biscuits in silver paper and an advertisement. During the war these were replaced by photographs of members of the staff who were serving in the forces.

In the warehouse, the further along the passage you went, the older the building. The floors were sloping and the ceilings lower. There was a smell and an atmosphere which was peculiar to that particular building. On the other side of the yard the cottages, which were put up by William, were now made into warehouses. They were for hardware: paint, brushes, pans, shovels and many other items. My mother's wash-house was now used as a store for empty boxes, and the upstairs of our house was turned into offices, a rest room for the staff, and toilets. The third storey put up by my grandfather was partly taken away but the roof was not as low as on the original premises, leaving some of the new bricks at the top.

This is a list taken from the 1936 price list showing the very many areas that were served by the travellers and lorries. During the Second World War some of the outlying areas such as Howden were dropped because of lack of petrol and were never restarted.

'COLLECTION AND DELIVERY OF ORDERS

Regularly can be relied on.

Arras, Belby, Bellasize, Bennetland, Bielby, Blacktoft, Brantingham, Broomfleet, Brough, Bubwith, Burnby, Bursea, Cave North, Cave South, Cliffe North and South, Crockey Hill, Dalton Holme, Dalton South, Drewton, Eastrington, Ellerker, Elloughton, Enthorpe, Escrick, Etton, Everingham, Everthorpe, Faxfleet, Foggathorpe, Gilberdyke, Good-manham, Harlthorpe, Harswell, Hasholme, Hayton, Hive, Holme on Spalding Moor, Hotham, Hotham Carr, Howden, Hunsley, Kilnwick (Nr. Driffield), Kiplingcotes, Little Weighton, Lockington, Londesborough, Londesborough Wold, Lund, Market Weighton Common, Melbourne, Metham, Middleton on the Wolds, Newbald, Newport, North Duffield, Nunburnholme, Riplingham Grange etc., Sancton, Sandholme, Seaton Ross, Shipton-thorpe, Skidby, Skipwith, Sleights (Howden), Spaldington, Saddlethorpe, Thornton, Thorpe-le-Street, Walkington, Warter Wold, Welton, Wheldrake, Willitoft, Yokefleet.

Customers will find it an advantage to have as complete a list as possible, in readiness for our traveller's call.'

It could make quite a good exercise for people, young and old to find all these villages and areas on a large scale map, as several are unfamiliar to me.

The business employed about 30 people but in 1939, during the Second World War, many things changed. Most of the men and some of the girls were called up. There was, however, the Hebden family who looked after the warehouses. This comprised Tom Hebden, respectfully known as 'Mr. Hebden' as he was the foreman, and under him were Cyril and Sidney, his two sons. The three of them worked at the shop for very many years, and, when his father retired, Cyril became foreman and then took the name of 'Mr. Hebden'. There were also other men who were not called up for various reasons: Walter Playforth, Percy Beal, Albert Metcalfe, George Bell, Willie Yates, Jim Machen, and John Henry Smith. In those days the girls were not called by their Christian names. They were called 'Miss or Mrs. Smith', but the men were called by their surnames unless they were travellers or head of a department. It all seems very strange today when most people are called by their Christian names whatever position they hold.

Girls who worked in the shop.

Some of the girls from the shop.

A tradition in Market Weighton which finished when the war began took place on new year's day each year. All the children congregated outside the various grocers, shouting: 'Oi! Oi! Oi!' and nuts or sweets were thrown out to them. My father thought this unfair as usually the stronger children grabbed the most. At our shop the children were told to queue up and each child was given an orange, an apple or, once, a little tin of biscuits. I have often wondered how many children rejoined the end of the queue. This tradition still exists in Driffield.

Rationing became a nightmare and made much more work, not only for the office staff but for those who served behind the counter. Mr. Percy Beal, who stayed during the war, was in charge of the front shop, and girls who travelled from the outlying villages often struggled through deep snow in order to get to work or sometimes stayed at our house until conditions improved. The small rations meant weighing up minute quantities of fat, butter, margarine, sugar and bacon etc., particularly for single householders or small families, and was more work for less money.

The plum trees in the garden were pulled up and a large air raid shelter was put on the right of the path. Further down the garden the staff used the land as allotments to help their families and to 'Dig for Victory'. The old 'Top Office', which had been my father's before 1933 when he moved into the main office block and had laid empty for about six years, suddenly took on a new importance. My father became chairman of the Market Weighton Invasion Committee. This entailed much planning in case the enemy decided to land in this country and particularly on the North East coast. Market Weighton was to be taken as an example for the whole country and was consequently visited by important army, naval and airforce chiefs. The 'Top Office' was wallpapered in maps and other documents, and was the headquarters for the important 'Invasion Committee'. Many of the more secret meetings took place in the dining room of our home on Londesborough Road and I can remember helping to carry in the supper to many high-ranking officers.

Each morning my father would send out notices to the different departments of the shop so that the staff were informed of any changes. I was lucky to be given a copy of some of these, and this is a selection:

EXTRACTS FROM THE MORNING PAPERS

1939 December 16th
FARTHINGS – Controlled Maximum Prices.
Where old farthings appear in the controlled prices – as in Milk 9¼d. and 7¼d. – They are not allowed to be treated as ½d. Otherwise the ¼d. must be charged.

1940 September 28th
Owing to enemy action only a very small range of Kemps biscuits is available, and in limited quantities.

1940 December 24th
Once more – A HAPPY XMAS – and let us, in our festivities, give a thought to those of our old workmates who cannot be home for Xmas. Harry West will be on guard all day and probably others likewise.

1941 January 16th
TEA – The printing works of the firm supplying and packing our tea has been destroyed by enemy action. For the time being, therefore, they will be unable to supply the same design of bag. We have good stocks packed in our usual designs.

1941 March 14th
BLOOD TRANSFUSION – I am proud of the fact that ten out of the first 61 enrolled are either from here or Tel-el-Fara.

1941 March 19th
RETAIL SALES (PAPER WRAPPING) – It is an offence under the Control of Paper (No. 28) Order to wrap or pack with paper any article which does not reasonably require any such wrapping or packing for its protection.
SOAP – Owing to the shortage of suitable paper and of the cutting down of newspaper, the wrapping of soap, other than Toilet Soap which may come unwrapped, will be discontinued.

1941 May 9th
GAS MASKS – A previous request has been made that these shall be brought to work by everyone. This request has been complied with by some but ignored by many. It must therefore be taken as a definite order that they shall be brought to work.
At certain times the whole staff will be required to wear their respirators for ten minutes whilst carrying on their usual work.
BRING YOUR RESPIRATOR TOMORROW AND EVERY DAY.

1941 June 4th
DOG BISCUITS – From today, all Dog Biscuits will be allocated to customers in rotation as supplies become available. For this purpose each traveller and the shop are requested to pass in a list of pre-war regular buyers of Dog Biscuits. This is urgent as we have a supply awaiting allocation. No allocation will be made until the list is reasonably complete.
OATS AND ROLLED OATS must now be sold only as Horse Feed against Horse Feed Coupons or counterfoils, and we have to give a written undertaking to this effect.

1941 November 20th
ONIONS – The first issue at ½ lb. is invoiced. Lists are being prepared for each journey and for the shop. In the latter case, the necessary entry (which will be explained) must be made BEFORE supplying the onions.

1941 November 21st
CONTROL OF PAPER ORDER – It has now been made quite clear that only food stuffs may be wrapped up. No paper must be used for any other purpose, nor must parcels etc. be labelled unless it is impossible for the particulars required to be written on the article or parcel itself.

1942 January 8th
PAPER BAGS – Please make an appeal to customers to take care of, and return used bags. So far as possible these will be used only for feeding stuffs and potatoes, new bags being reserved for flour. The position is acute, so please do all you can to get as many back as possible.

1942 March 12th
FLOUR – We must do our utmost to share our white flour equitably between our registered customers. Please, therefore, make a special effort to prevent any person getting more than their average weekly or fortnightly quantity.

1942 June 17th
LIBYA – Let us all remember especially, in these anxious days, not only those who may be in battle, but also their loved ones who are working with us here. HWL

1942 July 11th
Please remind all to bring their respirators on Monday. On this occasion I want you ALL to put on your

respirators at 5.30 pm and carry on your usual work in them. Try to stick it for the full half hour.

1942 August 5th
APPLES – Please mention to customers that they require a Food Office Licence to sell apples of their own growing by retail. All apples of less than 2" diameter must be kept separate – maximum retail 4½d. per lb. (Larger apples 8d. lb.)

1942 September 4th
Respirators will be worn from 5.30 pm to 6 pm this evening.

1942 December 18th
CHOCOLATE BISCUITS – For shop only – No customer who has had them from a traveller may have another lot, nor may country customers who give an order through the traveller. Country have previously had their allocation and will get them again as soon as sufficient are accumulated.

NOTE – NO CHOCOLATE BISCUITS may be supplied without making reference to and crossing the name off the allocation list.

1943 April 13th
MATCHES – We can carry through the fortnight at TWO boxes for larger orders but only ONE for smaller orders. Town and Shop must not exceed one per week. Weekly allocation will be given to shop by T. H. each Monday and may not be exceeded.

1943 May 4th
FLOUR – It is now compulsory to keep a record of all retail sales of 28lb. To comply with this requirement, you must make out a bill and duplicate EVEN FOR A CASH SALE for any quantity over 28lb.

1943 May 5th
CURRANTS – Each traveller may sell today only as allocation slip – limit half-pound (30 x ½lb. each traveller). Twelve points per pound.

1943 October 15th
ORANGES – 7½d. per lb. (Allocation No. 1). 2lb. against Green Books – see instructions. 1lb. against Blue Books. (until other instructions are received. Mark the Allocation number on 2-panel outside back cover.)

1943 October 29th
BLACK-OUT – Shop and stairs – including small window near biscuit stand must be blacked out every night, commencing TOMORROW Saturday. Back Shop and Offices to be blacked out on and from MONDAY night.

1944 February 1st
WILLIE WARD – It is with deep regret that we hear that he is missing – but I'm sure we all trust that – even if in enemy hands – we may hear that he is safe. (Unfortunately he had died.)

1944 February 22nd
BLACK-OUT TONIGHT 6.51 pm.
LEMONS – Limit strictly to two lemons per house – must be weighed and charged at 6½d. per lb. Shop sales must be crossed off allocations list to prevent unfair buying. 'TOWN Journey' customers will get theirs through travellers today and tomorrow. Prices to be left open on bills.

1944 October 7th
SHOP BLACK-OUT – If we are to avoid erecting the 'Black-out Passage' it will be essential to see that the shop doors are not left standing open after dark. At Black-out, lock the Grocery side door and use the Provision side door.

1944 December 12th
DRIED FRUIT – Supplementary Allocation, commenced Monday Dec 11th ½lb. fruit and ½lb. dates per Sugar Registration. There is no surplus. Currants are in ¼lb only – limit one – and to those with three registrations or over.

Note that ¼lb Currants counts as ½lb Fruit – i.e. one person's ration.

1945 January 24th
STARCH – 4d. size – may be sold (limit one to registered customers only).
CAMP – Coffee and Chicory 11½ d and 1s. 10d. – may be sold to registered customers only.
TOILET SOAP – With strict limit of one tablet to registered customers only (2 tabs for large orders).
POTATOES 1st. – to registered customers only IS ABSOLUTE MAXIMUM.

1945 January 26th
JAM – Strawberry 1s., Raspberry 1s., Blackcurrant 1s. All in stock but note specially, only ONE single jar of these varieties (NOT one of each) may be entered on any order EXCEPT two jars (in all) may be entered where there is a rating of four or over. This must be strictly observed.

1945 March 3rd
BISCUITS – It must be clear that the TOTAL LIMIT is now ½lb. only. There are many orders where ½lb. plain and ½lb. Choc. Biscuits have been entered.

The only exception to the ½lb. limit are in orders with a rating of FIVE or over – or – in a case of genuine illness the addition of ½lb. of Cream Crackers.

1945 May 12th V-E DAY May 8th
I want to say a sincere thank you to all for the way in which the work has been brought up to date following VE-day. It has been a real tonic. So again, Thank you.

1945 August 14th
V.J. DAY – Attention is called to the provisional arrangements for dealing with Country orders. It is hoped to avoid opening the shop on either of the two days holiday, but this will depend on circumstances. *NB* At midnight it was announced that Wednesday was to be V.J. Day.

1945 September 18th
CUSTARD POWDER – Allocation Monday, Tuesday, Wednesday – custard powder tins on all other orders, you may enter from four 1½d. to eight 1½d. pkts.

SOAP RATIONING – Now based on Coupon K on Page 15 of Ration Book, which MUST now be cut out. Remember that our future supplies depend entirely on the coupons that you bring in NOW. No soap, whether hard, powder, flakes or toilet must go out unless the appropriate COUPONS are cut out.

1945 December 15th
A HEARTY WELCOME TO CHAS. ALLINSON on his return to us after almost 5½ years absence on Military Service.

1946 January 8th

Mr. R. L. GREEN – We extend a welcome to Leslie Green on his return from over five years service in the forces.

1946 February 1st

MATCHES – MAY BE SOLD in Town this week.

SOAP – Coupons for period 8 are worth ONLY THREE RATIONS (except for those from the Child's Green Books which are worth four rations).

TEA – Period 8. The ration is HALF A POUND per person and all sales should be in multiples of this quantity.

STARCH – 8 x 1lb. for Arras orders only 10d. per lb. STARCH may be entered on Town orders today and tomorrow only. 9½d. for 20 pkts and 4d. for 60 pkts.

1946 February 8th

MATCHES – Do NOT sell in Town this week.

Town only for each customer either Custard Powder 3 x 1½d. or Greens Chocolate Mould 4½d.

1946 February 13th

TOILET SOAP – NONE. The nearest approach is Family Health 4oz. tablets at 2½d.

1946 March 1st

MRS. ELLA – Tonight we say 'au-revoir' to Mrs. Ella as a member of our Staff. Whilst thanking her for her good work throughout her stay with us, I am sure that you will all join with me in wishing her and her husband the utmost happiness in the years ahead.

* * *

How easily we have forgotten all these shortages.

There were also many messages sent by the members of staff in the forces who regularly sent letters to my father.

I am including here a letter sent to my sisters and me during the war from my father. It came after the heavy bombing of Hull:

May 11th 1941

Thank you for all your letters this week.

You will have been wondering how we have fared since Wednesday night.

Well, we are all all right – though tired – and nothing dropped within seven miles or so.

I am writing this at the office (10.40 am). Playforth and I have been slicing bread and cheese on the bacon slicers for the evacuees.

Wednesday night and Thursday night were terrible (in the distance). The whole district was lighted by some of the flashes and the glow of fire stretched for far enough over Mrs. Dinsdale's house.

Joyce – It's a good thing you got your coat from Thornton's – for theirs, Hammond's, Bladon's and many, many others just don't exist – including the huge Co-op building on Jameson Street.

Rank's Mills among others and White's Sugar Mills are completely demolished.

I understand a bomber with its full load crashed on Hammond's.

For the past few days the traffic through Market Weighton in both directions has been ceaseless, army lorries, empty buses, fire brigades and ambulances, mobile canteens etc. going in. Loaded buses, cars, lorries etc. coming back.

Fire brigades etc. from further away than you are (Derbyshire), have been coming through, and I believe the fires were only got under control 7 pm Saturday night.

At 10 pm Friday night the first bus loads of evacuees begun to arrive – the most pitiful bundles of humanity – old folk, children etc.

'Ethel's Chapel' (Primitive Methodist) was first filled, then the Boys' School.

Fortunately we and the Co-op had put fire watchers on and they were able to help with collecting and slicing bread etc..

These had got settled in when a message came that another two double decker bus loads were on the way. I ran Mrs. Evans (Vicar's wife) round in the car rousing helpers for the Girls' School and Catholic School and whilst we were up Cliffe Road I saw the bus arrive at the Catholic School.

Helpers arrived quickly and 90 poor souls trooped out of the bus, including many children, hungry, weary and bewildered – many had had no sleep for nights and had lost all.

'Why are we stopping?'

'Where are we?'

'Where are we going?' came from one after the other. Eventually they got settled on the floor, on forms and desks. Not enough blankets to go round at one each. A few lucky children on old mattresses.

All – or most of them – so cheerful. Odd ones who had lost husbands were naturally upset.

One girl had dashed from bed in her pyjamas on Wednesday night, just putting on a pair of slacks and a coat. Whilst she was in the shelter, her bedroom was hit. She went to her mother's on Thursday and that night it too got a direct hit and all she had was her clothing of the night before.

Others had been dug out of the ruins of their homes.

Thursday nights fires were worse even than Wednesday's – in the night an immense red glow – in the daytime a dense column of smoke covering a wide area could be seen from here and even with all this they had the utmost difficulty to persuade the people to leave what was left and come out here.

On Friday night your mother was first at the Boys' School and later at the Girls' School until 6 am Saturday. She was on duty at the Boys' School again 2 pm to 6 pm and is there again this afternoon (Sunday).

Mrs. Evans is working like a trooper.

By the way – I only got the first page written at the office because we had other things to get ready and I am on phone duty at home this afternoon.

I was running about until 3 am Saturday from soon after tea on Friday. Then on and off all day Saturday we were slicing bread and doing other things.

At 10.30 pm. I was taking bread, tea, sugar, margarine etc. round and got to bed about midnight. I slept solidly until Gladys woke me at 8 am and I had to dash as I had promised to be at the shop by 9 am

Quite a lot of evacuees returned to Hull by bus, train lorry etc. yesterday but some came back very sorry that they had gone.

A fireman in a brigade from Coventry said that Coventry was bad but it was nothing to what Hull had got.

Molly Farmer rang up to say they evacuated all patients from the Infirmary without loss, but all around is, I believe, a shambles. ...

I may have to go into Hull tomorrow to see about flour and meal. I tried all yesterday to get them on the phone but it was hopeless. Their main office was moved to a country house at the outbreak of war (i.e. Rank's). They have lost mills also at Southampton, London and I believe South Wales.

Going out now. I don't think it will be any use your attempting to ring us up for the time being.

The blackout also must have caused difficulties at the shop, but, as we took this very much for granted, it is not something I particularly remember. Outside the next-door premises, which was the shop and workroom of Edith Davis, later Mrs. Kelsey, a tailoress, there was a large concrete road block which came so far across the pavement that if a pram was being wheeled along the footpath a diversion had to be made on to the road. This barrier was erected so that if there was an invasion the road could more easily be closed and guarded. I believe there was another somewhere on York Road.

Eventually the war was over and the staff came home and back to work at the shop. The air raid shelter was no longer needed and the blackout was removed. The Invasion Committee was disbanded. Rationing, however, was still there, until the 1950s.

In February 1959 the business and property were sold to Herbert Baldry, who was a potato wholesaler from Newbald who also had a fruit and vegetable shop further along the street. The shop front was once more changed and, instead of two doors and three windows, there was only one door and two windows. The name of Lyon was kept but the name on the front of the shop was 'Lyons'. Herbert Baldry made the offices above the shop into a restaurant.

The shop was turned into a supermarket and all the deliveries to both town and country were stopped. This completely altered the type of shop that had been in existence for very many years, but this was just a sign of the times and the old idea of 'service' which had meant so much to the old business was finished: also, we fear, a sign of the times.

In November 1965 Herbert Baldry had to cut down on work because of ill health and the doctor advised him to sell the business. Across the road was Walter Willson's, a Newcastle firm, who were finding their property too small and inconvenient as they had no back way to the shop. They bought the property from Herbert Baldry and carried on business there for seven years. In 1972 Walter Willson's wanted to close down the Market Weighton branch and sold to the Hull and East Riding Co-operative Society, which again moved from other premises in Northgate, which were not as central as that in Market Place. The café was closed and a flat made upstairs.

A considerable amount of building and demolition took place. Firstly the buildings on the west were pulled down to allow more room for big lorries and parking. Many of the doors and windows in the buildings on the east of the yard were bricked up and the shop was extended further back, making a much bigger shop more suitable for a supermarket. The cobbles in the yard, which originally came from old Hull, were covered with tarmac. The long garden has become a wilderness, or a nature reserve, whichever way you want to think of it, and the wall at the end is falling down. Children living beyond it will still enjoy the beck but will no longer find baby carrots floating down it. Houses were built in the field behind in Scott's Croft, which had also once been the venue for the Market Weighton show. In 1995 a new roof was put on the buildings, which were falling into poor repair and with a leaking roof. A new shop front in the same style was installed and now bears the name ' STOP & SHOP'.

One cannot help wondering what changes will be made in the next hundred years. As I listen to the news in November 1999, I hear of the amazing idea of housewives sending their grocery orders into supermarkets by the Internet. The new idea they say! The Internet may be new, but delivery of goods to the house is certainly not and I am sure our staff in the back shop would not make the mistakes which apparently are occurring at the moment with this 'new' method.

Baldry's shop front.

Shop front, 1996.

Interior Co-op, 1993.

SERVICES

WATER

At the junction of Cliffe and Sancton roads near the Catholic church and on Market Hill could be seen a pump which supplied many households. There was also one on The Green. Resting on a long wooden arm was a long leather hose for filling water carts belonging to farmers and the water cart for watering the streets of the town to keep down the dust. Some houses had their own well and pump in the back yard.

The well in the yard at St. Catherine's Nursing Home is enormous and beautifully built with brick arches. When it was a private house belonging to a nursery-man, John Proudlock, a servant had to stand in the kitchen and pump the water up to a very big wooden, but lead-lined, water tank in the roof. This would only be used once a bathroom was built and installed some time after the house was built, possibly early 1900. The bath installed at the time was very big but unfortunately the hot water tank put in much later only allowed enough hot water to give about two inches in the bottom. The lavatory was on a platform and, although very unhygienic, was very prettily decorated with blue daffodils inside and had on the back the word 'TRIUMPH', a very appropriate name. The chain had on it a white knob which gave the instruction to those who were unfamiliar with such modern conveniences – 'PULL'. I know all this because we lived there when it was called The Hollies. This extension had no foundations and, falling away from the main building, was demolished when the nursing home built on a new wing.

All these pumps have disappeared and maybe it is better that we don't have to use them. On the Market Hill the pump was of concern to the Council. In fact the people of the town today would be amazed if the Council gave out the following announcement about their water supply:

In January 1895 — 'Vice Chairman Sherwood has taken under his wing the future of the Market Weighton Town Pump. This imposing(?) looking structure bearing the inscription "WATER PURE AND FREE" has for some unknown reason refused to furnish any further supply. At the next Council meeting Councillor Sherwood intends to handle the matter.'

In June 1895 Mr. Sapcote proposed that the council ask the Sanitary

The old pump on the Green.

The Hollies, Londesborough Road, 1979.

Committee to take samples of the water at Market Weighton both from the pump on Market Hill and from the Water Company's supply and have it analysed. In July 1895 the results were available.

At the Council meeting the report on the analysis of water from the District Council was read. It concluded that 'the pipe on the Market Hill was too near the bottom of the well and suggested that the well be deepened and a bent spout be added so as to

Pump on Market Hill.

The water pumping station, Springwells.

Goodmanham Mill.

prevent anything being put into it. It was no use having it cut as only a short piece was usable.' But Councillor Sherwood had obviously done a satisfactory job because it was said at a later meeting:

'The Market Weighton pump question – The Pump Committee of the Parish Council met Mr. Villiers of Beverley on Thursday who thoroughly examined the Market Hill pump. The pump was put in operation and an extraordinary flow was found. Samples of the water were taken with the purpose of analysis.'

As a result the Market Hill pump water was pronounced pure and that produced by the Water Company stated to be of exceptionally good quality.

A newspaper reported:

'The long-talked-of Market Hill pump has again been put in proper order. The pump has been put up by subscription. Mr. Kelsey, many thanks.'

The water works at Springwells was constructed in 1884 or 1885. The Market Weighton water order document stated:

'A well or shaft and boring with headings and a tank and pumping station, with engines and other works, to be wholly situated in a field in the said parish of Market Weighton belonging to the Right Honourable Lord Londesborough opposite to the Spring Plantation.'

Interestingly it refers to the pipes crossing the lane to Goodmanham nearer Market Weighton, called Hull Street. It had been a Roman road from Brough. We called this lane Red Lane as it was made up with crushed brick from the brick works which used to be close by and was always red until it was covered with tarmac and widened when the secondary school was built.

At the same time there was an objection from the North Eastern Railway Company, at that time the owners of the mill at the bottom of this lane. Although it had been a windmill, it was also a water mill. The owners were worried that the flow of water to turn the mill would be depleted when the people of Market Weighton started obtaining their water from Springwells. The two springs called Goodmanham Spring and Crunkhill Spring situated near the well or shaft and pumping station supplied the water which flowed down the beck and worked the mill. The reservoir for the water at Springwells is still at the top of the hill nearby and is a steep climb to reach. There is now another reservoir beyond the school playing fields on Beverley Road.

But now we no longer need to carry water from the pump, be it on Southgate, Market Hill, The Green or even in the backyard of the house, however 'PURE AND FREE' it may be.

In the *Howdenshire Gazette* in 1900 appeared the following article:

'Sanitary Conditions.
Great improvements had been made in the matter of cleanliness, removal of refuse etc. The cowkeepers premises were clean and well kept. From a sanitary point of view there were many things yet to find fault with, but the favourable conditions at Weighton of good water, efficient drainage and plenty of ventilation of pure air rendered the unsanitary state of some yards innocuous. In densely populated areas such insanitary conditions would not be allowed to exist. He referred especially to the nearness of privies and piggeries to many of the cottages and the close proximity of foldyards to the public streets.'

Even many years later there were still foldyards in the centre of the town: one immediately behind the church, another in Finkle Street at the beginning of what is now Hill Rise, and also in Southgate. A dairy farm with foldyard and a pig farm was situated near Market Hill and I am sure there were more.

Because of the dusty roads a water cart was used to water the streets. In 1901 it was resolved that the Water Company be asked the sum they would charge per load of 250 gallons as it was considered this would be more economical and avoid time spent filling the water cart on The Green. On consulting the chairman and engineer of the Water Company, it was found that this plan would be impractical as it would be necessary for the engineer to be present when hydrants were used.

Copeland's foldyard behind the church.

High Street, about 1890. The streets were very dusty.

seems strange today to think that it was so important to water the streets, but at that time they were not finished with tarmac, and, even later, in 1911, there was a report in the newspaper as follows:

'It was said that the night soil from Hull was continually coming into the station and carted away through the town with liquid running out of the bottom of the cart to the annoyance caused to the inhabitants of Market Weighton by the reason of night soil being carted through the streets of the town in the hours of daylight and that the same is injurious to the health of the town which they wanted stopping. At the Council meeting Councillor Kirby said he was in sympathy with Mr. Wadsworth's motion but seeing the great quantity of night soil that annually came into the station consigned to various farmers in the district, in many cases who live several miles away in the district, which would necessitate them having to leave their home very early in the morning and at a time of the year long before daylight to enable them to get the night soil off the rail and through the town before the specified time and in many cases would be unsuccessful'

In 1902, as the pump on The Green was out of order, it was decided that –

'the same be put into working order forthwith, that the spreader on the water cart be cleaned, that William Drake should water the streets for the present at last year's rate of payment viz. 1s. per load and that he should water the streets to the following points:
Southgate – Mr. George Kelsey's house at the end of the town. Holme Road- Miss Rowntree's house, Shipton Road – Mr. Winter's house. Hungate – Mr. Maynard's house. Londesborough Road – The station gates. Beverley Road – Mr. Sykes' house.'

A temporary arrangement was made to water the streets at a payment of 1s. per load. As eight or ten loads were used in one day, at this rate the funds at the disposal of the Council for this purpose would soon be exhausted. About this time it was arranged with the Water Company that stand pipes with a tap would be erected. Standpipes were to be situated, one behind the pump and the other behind the telegraph pole, at the corner of Southgate. This work would cost £7. It

No wonder the streets needed watering. I would have thought they needed swilling – and yet we now grumble at the smell of pig slurry from the fields.

Market Weighton Parish Council was not formed until 1895. Meetings were usually held in the Girls' School in Hungate. The councillors were elected by the people of Market Weighton.

The following is a list of the candidates with the number of votes they were given in late 1894:

MARKET WEIGHTON COUNCIL
Councillors

Barker Robert	39	Barnes George	50
Bell George	68	Dunhill Henry Everit	62
Elliot John Henry	26	French Robert Digby	61
Haigh John William	57	Holmes William	62
Hudson John	44	Hyde Francis	58
Inglis James Brown	56	Jefferson Thomas Jewison	72
Johnson William	40	Kelsey George Jun.	58
Lyon Thomas Green	52	Potter Frank	60
Roantree Kirk	43	Proudlock John	48
Sapcote Abraham Fredk.	69	Sherwood John	53
Simpson Richard	47	Vickers Tom	22
Wake Peter	92	Watson Henry	11
Wilson Joseph Johnson	36		

FIRE BRIGADE

Once the parish councils were started in 1895 it appears that they ran the fire brigades. Previously they were sometimes financed by the insurance companies and fire engines would not be taken to a fire if the premises was not insured. Sometimes the fire engine was supplied and run by the Vestry.

When the Great Fire of London broke out in the early hours, in September 1666, there were no organised groups of men to fight the fire and it was not until 1680 that the first fire insurance company called simply Fire Office was established in London. The idea grew more popular and companies realised the need to employ trained officers and so more privately owned fire brigades were formed to put out fires in the properties they insured. Very crude fire engines were in existence from the early seventeenth century but were rare. The men employed wore arm badges and were also supplied with distinctive uniforms in the colours of the company.

I have a record of what is likely to have been the first fire engine in Market Weighton. This was very early for a town of this size. A. J. Compton Merryweather of 4 Whitehall Court, London SW recalls in the 1914 *Yorkshire Herald*, the following entry in the books of his firm:

> 'Township of Market Weighton, Yorks.
> Ordered per Mr. R. Dalton, Bank, Beverley
> May 12th 1821 – A new 2nd size (Patent) Fire Engine, with metallic pistons and valves, mounted on strong spoke wheels with forecarriage made to lock under the cistern and shafts complete. The whole of the best materials and finished in the most substantial manner, painted green and vermilion. Including new length of suction pipe complete.
> One length of strong leather hose 40 feet with brass screws.
> One ditto 29 feet with ditto
> Packing the engine etc. in a strong deal case cartage to Beal's Wharf.
> Insuring the engine etc. from risk at sea, etc. at Royal Exchange Assurance Office.'

You will notice the engine was sent to its destination by sea. There were no railways then. It is said that the journey from London took three days.

The Lighting and Watching Act (1820) allowed money to be available to the church for such things as fire engines. It was thought that this is why the 1821 fire engine had been sent to Market Weighton, but, having looked through the church records at the Borthwick Institute in York, I found no evidence for this theory.

In Baines directory for 1823, I found that a Mr. Robert Dalton was the manager of the Royal Exchange Assurance Company, whose offices, along

MARKET WEIGHTON FIRE ENGINE.

This apparatus was employed in combating the fire at Grange Farm. It is a manual fire engine, believed to be over 100 years old and not very efficient.

Fire engine, 1914.

Royal Exchange Badge.

with those of a bank, were at North Bar Within, Beverley, possibly the reason why his address was just recorded in the records of A. J. Compton Merryweather as 'Mr. R. Dalton, Bank, Beverley'.

The Royal Exchange Assurance applied for a charter to undertake fire insurance, which was eventually granted, and it began underwriting fire risks in May 1721. It was a hundred years later when more people were insuring their property that the insurance company must have decided to supply Market Weighton with this engine to protect its customers. Amazingly the only insurance companies with an office in this town at that time were Atlas and County and no office appeared for Royal Exchange Assurance in the following years. Houses which were insured by a particular company had to have on their wall a special badge and each had its own number. Some are still to be seen on buildings today, but as far as I know there are none left in Market Weighton. The badge in the copy shown is for the years 1810-1838, which could be the one that the people of Market Weighton would have fastened to their buildings. It measured 22.2 x 10.5 cm and showed the central tower and main entrance of the Royal Exchange.

May 1895 the *Howdenshire Gazette* reported:

'On Friday afternoon week a fire broke out in one of the outbuildings of Mr. Ramsey's saddler's establishment at Market Weighton. The shed contained a boiler on the ground floor and up above was used for storing horse collars, packing etc. and it is probable that, whilst boiling operations were going on below, a spark had ignited the stuff above and, but for the promptitude of the workmen on the place and of the fire brigade under the command of Captain Wright, considerable damage would have been done. Obtaining water from the hydrant, the "Manuel" sent a good supply of water on the building, and after removing part of the roof the fire was checked and extinguished after doing damage, it is roughly estimated, to the extent of about £50.'

The 'Manuel' which seemed very satisfactory according to the newspaper report of Mr. Ramsey's fire, would be the one bought in 1821, but, in spite of this, at a Council meeting in July 1895 Mr. French complained that at a recent fire the engine was found to be leaking and the hose pipe was of no use, it having had to be cut and only a short piece being usable. Dr. Jefferson proposed that a committee be formed and approved to inspect the hose and see what was best, the committee to be empowered to purchase a new hose if necessary. In October 1895 the committee elected to investigate the fire engine and see what might be refitted to put it into good working order and were of the opinion that it would cost £20, with the hose, and also to have a new bottom put in the engine. Rev. French proposed that the work be done as early as possible, it being a necessary requirement.

In November 1895 in response to a notice published by the new Market Weighton Parish Council, asking for volunteers to form a fire brigade, the following responded:

Brown Ernest	Charter William
Grantham William	Grantham Jun. I.
Greenwood Frederic	Harrison George
Hudson John	Hyde Frank
Lent James	Kneeshaw William
Mizon Alfred	Sapcote Abraham
Sapcote Thomas	Smalley Robert
Scab George (farmer)	Winter Henry
Wright Ernest.	

Market Weighton seems to have been very advanced with its Fire Brigades as in 1897 Bridlington had only a Manuel fire engine and only one man in charge of it. They either had to wire Scarborough or look for voluntary help when a fire broke out.

In March 1896, when there was a terrible fire at Messrs. Grant and English's warehouse in Pocklington, there was no fire engine in that town and all that could be used until York steam fire engine

arrived ('pulled at the gallop by four horses'), were buckets. Notice had been sent to Market Weighton and Beverley but for some reason they never arrived. Market Weighton had already had a Manuel fire engine for 75 years by this time.

A newspaper article in April 1896 stated:

'The Market Weighton Fire Brigade do not admit that they were summoned to the Pocklington blaze, and yet they received a telegram countermanding the alleged summons to come to Pocklington. We have received a long private letter on the subject in which the writer deprecates the action of some anonymous correspondent who wanted to know why the summons had not been responded to. Until a summons has been proved, it was certainly unjust to condemn the Market Weighton Fire Brigade, who, we are sure, would have done all in their power to render assistance to their neighbours in distress.'

In October 1898 the Fire Brigade Committee produced a report which asked for a supply of caps, hand lamps, buckets and extra hose. Those were to be supplied. I have no more information until September 1901 when farmers were told that, if they had a fire and wanted the fire engine, they had to supply two horses fully harnessed for conveyance of the fire engine.

March 1901 The following accounts presented to the council:

George Playforth (catching 12 moles)	3s. 0d.
William Hunter (work done to engine shed)	£1. 10s. 10d.
S. H. Cooper (lamps for fire brigade)	6s. 4d.
James Milne and Son (new stand pipe)	£4. 11s. 3d.

In January 1903 it was reported that, because the Parish Councils of Goodmanham and Shipton would not enter into an arrangement to allow them to have the fire brigade in case of a fire, and pay, the Council would not guarantee that the fire engine would attend fires there.

In 1914 a fire broke out at The Grange, a farm belonging to Mr. George Stather. The whole of the contents of the Dutch barn were burnt out, it was said, because the Market Weighton fire engine was so inefficient. Not surprising, when it was 93 years old.

The Lighting Committee, which had the question of the fire engine under consideration for some considerable time, reported that, after various inspections and exhibitions by the brigade, they recommended that after the miserable display they had seen they considered that a new engine should be obtained and the Clerk be instructed to ascertain the probable cost.

At a later meeting, the Clerk read correspondence with Messrs. Merryweather. The committee favoured the firm's recommendation to purchase an engine quoted at £98. Some amusement was caused by the Clerk's enquiry whereas the old engine could be taken in 'part exchange'; the firm had suggested that it might be presented to some local troop of Boy Scouts. It had been purchased in 1821 and the firm feared they could not make any allowance on it.

The building next to the old police station on The Green used to be used by the Territorials before it was taken over as a fire station. This remained in use for that purpose until April 1967 when the new large fire

Market Weighton Fire Brigade competition, late 1920s.
George Dobson, ?, A. Saltmer, Harold Bristow, Allan Johnson, Cyril Hebden,
J. W. Kneeshaw, Bill Moore, Harold Lyon, Sir R. Walker, ?, Jack Harrison

Fire Brigade early 1940s
Bill Moore, Charles Frankish, Bill Collins, Arthur Harrison, Allan Johnson,
Cyril Hebden, George Priestman, Frank Watson, George Petch.

During the war there were two 5,000-gallon tanks of water for use in the town in case of fire. Market Weighton was lucky as Pocklington had none, though it would use the beck. One of these tanks was situated on The Green and the other off York Road where cottages had been pulled down and where the market is in 1999.

After 1946 the old 'air raid siren' was used to summon the firemen but I have been told by an old fireman that in days gone by a bell was fastened to a high pole in the Half Moon yard where the fire engine was kept. Later the bell was fastened to the fire station on The Green. Communication with the fire-men is much more individual now and little boys, and big ones too, have no time to jump on their bikes when the bell or siren goes and race after the engine.

My father was very much involved with the fire brigade and he would tell the story of one night when one of the firemen went with a match to find a leak in the acetylene lamp. The result can be imagined. I was told that they then had to put out a fire on the fire engine. His horses were used at one time for pulling the fire engine and later his Daimler lorry. He used to say he never begrudged the time his men who were also in the fire brigade were away from work, however inconvenient, as one time it could be his shop or his home that needed them.

Summer 1995: Market Weighton firemen revisit their heritage (the old station on The Green). As can be seen, fire engines have got bigger and bigger: it is difficult to imagine that two appliances fitted into this station. Neil Mizon, Dave Sissons, Maurice Thorpe, Kevin Freer, Anthony Richardson, Garry Saltmer, John Speak, Paul Richardson, Pete Binns, Brian Crabtree, John McCune, Laurence Simpkins, Keith Lowe, Vince Worral.

station opened on Cliffe Road enabling larger fire engines to be used. During the war a prefabricated building was erected at the south side of The Green with accommodation for the firemen. Many of them slept there when on duty, and it served for operational use, as office, drying room etc. until 1967 when it was taken over by the Market Weighton Young Farmers as a club room before at last being demolished. It was one of the few places which needed to be pulled down as it was an eyesore and was getting very dilapidated, having been put up as a temporary building.

Before the days of fire engines, however primitive, the only way of fighting fires was by the use of buckets and hand 'squirts' to project the water at the fire. The main implements were fire hooks, axes and ladders. The early buckets were made of leather, hand sewn and coated with pitch inside. How different from the large, fully equipped fire engines and well trained firemen of today. The engines are now so big that the old fire station would be useless, even for one. Much of the work undertaken by the firemen is involved in rescue work at accidents on the roads, and the amount of calls has increased dramatically. For example, in the period 1976 to 1983 the station responded to an average of 65 calls a year whilst in 1991 the number of calls had risen to 181. The Market Weighton force attend fires in areas further away, such as Pocklington, Brough and Beverley and are on stand-by for Hull.

John Speak fighting a bus fire at Holme on Spalding Moor.

Somebody told me that when he was a boy, living in Holme on Spalding Moor and attending the old school in the centre of the village, a fire had started when they went into school. The Market Weighton fire engine, pulled by horses, arrived as they went for their dinner. One can only think that either fires had been extinguished by other means, or the building or stack would be burnt down by the time somebody rode on horseback to inform the brigade, horses were found and harnessed up and the engine was pulled to the fire. How different from today.

LIGHTING

London was the first city in the world to be lit by gas in 1807. It would be much later before Market Weighton had this facility.

The Council looked after the street lights, lit each night by a 'lamp lighter' and turned off later in the evening. In January 1898 an account received from Market Weighton Gas Light and Coke Company for gas consumed in the streets amounted to £52. 19s. 8d.

In 1902 the Clerk was instructed to make arrangements with the Gas Company and also the lamplighter, the latter to be informed that he must clean the lamps every full moon. If there was a full moon the lamps were not lit as the moon gave more light than the lamps and saved fuel. This, of course, was the reason the lights were cleaned at that time. The lamp lighter probably had a day-time job as well.

I was told by an old Market Weighton man that:

'An old fellow used to go with a brazier over his shoulder like they did in olden days when they had a torch-light processions. He just used to press a little thing on each lamp and then light it. By the time he got round and before he went to bed he had to set off round again to put them out. Well, you know, if he had to go to Sancton Road and the end of Holme Road and York Road and everywhere, it would take him some time,

wouldn't it? It would be Hector Mitchell's father that I remember doing it.'

At a ratepayers' meeting in 1889 to consider how much should be spent on lighting the town there was a poor attendance because of bad weather, reported the *Howdenshire Chronicle*:

'Councillor Hollings presided at the meeting and Councillor Lyon (chairman of the Lighting Committee) said that there was no balance in hand and the estimated cost of gas for street lighting purposes was about £85 for the 34 weeks during which the lamps would be lit. The wages for the lamplighter at 10s a week would, with the cost of gas, make a total of £102. He proposed that the sum of £110 should be asked, which left £8 to meet expenses of the Fire Brigade. Complaints had been made about the time the lamps were put out. Some had been seen to be burning at half past twelve, but Councillor Lyon said that it took a long time for a man to go round, starting at eleven o'clock. He also pointed out that there were at least one third more lamps now than when £60 was voted some years before. It was decided that £110 be allowed.'

GAS

The gasworks in Market Weighton were built in 1847 by the York and North Midland Railway Company (later, North Eastern Railway Company). Gas was then used only for lighting and at one time it was thought that it might have been for the station only, but this has been disproved.

In February 1871, £2,000 worth of £1 shares, was raised by eleven local business men to form the Market Weighton Gas Light and Coke Co. Ltd. Its objectives were to purchase a gas works and a small portion of land adjoining it owned by the North Eastern Railway Company near the station, to erect a gasworks and to manufacture, store and sell gas, coke and coal to the people of Market Weighton. The deeds show that the railway company's gas works must have supplied more than the station buildings as, when the sale went through, there were meters, lamps, plant, washer, fixtures, gas pipes and other apparatus. The secretary was Foster Parkinson, a tallow chandler and broker, assistant overseer and surveyor, and agent for the Caledonian and Equitable Insurance Companies, who appeared at that time to live at the police house on The Green (possibly a lodger) and John Seaton West Kirkpatrick, a solicitor of Market Weighton. This original gas works is on or very near the new gas works. The deeds show the site had the school on one side, the police station on another, railway land (the lines) on the third and a pinfold on the fourth side. At this time a gentleman by the name of Ernest Wright, more than likely the one who was captain of the fire brigade, was manager. After this nothing appears to be recorded about the gas works until 1896-1898 when a major reorganisation took place.

Gasworks at Market Weighton.

When I was a child my father was chairman of this company and I was taken with him to the gas works. I remember being very frightened when the retorts were charged. This plant had two beds of five retorts 22 inches x 16 inches x 9 feet 6 inches overall, originally installed by Simneys of Halifax. These retorts had to be charged by hand every six hours. (The retort was the closed vessel in which gas was distilled from the coal.) There were also two gas holders for the storage of the gas.

I quote from an article written by Mr. K. O. M. Golisti, with his kind permission, for an explanation by me would be impossible. Having read this, I am not surprised that I was frightened, but at least it made me appreciate the dreadful job the stoker had. This process entailed:

'Filling and wheeling a barrow containing between one and two cwts. (50-101 kilos) of blended sized coal from the coal store to the

proximity of the retort setting. It was the responsibility of the stoker to carefully remove the closure lid of the retort, immediately igniting the escaping gas (to avoid the risk of gas accumulating in pockets and subsequent explosion). The next task was to remove the incandescent mass that lay at the bottom of the retort, by inserting an iron rake to the back of the mass and pulling it forward so that it fell either on the floor or into a barrow that had been placed below the mouth of the retort. The coke was then quenched with water. All these activities resulted in a mixture of heat, dust, smoke and gas, in short, a most unpleasant and unhealthy working environment. The constant exposure to coal dust and tar gave rise to cancer of the scrotum – legislation requiring regular medical examination was introduced in the 1930s. Protecting his face by the best means that could be thought of, he wheeled the barrow and the coke deposited out of the retort house. The stoker, facing the empty retort, began to shovel coal into it, the first shovelful going to the extreme back of the retort. Each subsequent shovelful fell slightly short of its predecessor, until the whole length was filled, apart from a

Showing the gas works and railway with the back of the school on the right of the picture. About 1921.

gap of about six inches above the coal layer. Whilst all this was taking place crude gas poured out, which the closing of the retort door stopped. With the closing of the door the carbonising cycle began.'

The thought of having to repeat this process for all of the ten retorts every six hours seems an unbearable task and one can realise why there was always a smell of gas near every gas works.

By 1939, when E. C. Brown was manager and H. Legge was secretary, 600 tons of coal were carbonised. There were four miles of gas mains, 75 public street lights with clock controllers (Gone was the lamp lighter by this time). There were 400 consumers out of a population of 2000, 60 cookers used gas and there were 20 gas fires in Market Weighton. With the start of the war the lights of Market Weighton were not allowed to be lit because of the blackout. In 1949, soon after nationalisation, the lights of the town were lit by electricity.

In 1957/58 the following trade from the local gas works was recorded: 68.00 therms of gas, 5.80 cwts. of coke and 11.50 gallons of tar all per ton of coal carbonated. The tar was used in the chemical industry and was a very profitable by-product. It was used locally for preserving wooden buildings and fences, giving a very black finish which provided long-lasting protection.

When the gas company became the North Eastern Gas Board in 1961, Market Weighton became one of twelve districts of Hull Group. After this, the gas was supplied from Hull and the manufacturing side of the Market Weighton gas works closed down. The holders were still used to store a supply of gas. During a 12-day period in August 1968 all gas appliances were modified for the use of natural gas and the Market Weighton gas works were finally closed down.

In the coal manager's house, which was situated close by, was a room used as an office, and at one time a show room. This was moved to Pocklington and manned for many years by Stanley Kneeshaw. Also working for the gas works and coal yard was a very small man always known as 'Little Isaac'. I have only found one person who knew his surname. It was 'Gorling' He lived in a little cottage on Finkle Street.

When the gas works and house were eventually demolished the land was left derelict. It cannot be used for housing as it could be contaminated. A large metal gate is still there marking its entrance, immediately opposite Manor Fields on Spring Road.

GRAVEYARDS

When the cemetery in Holme Road was opened the Council was responsible for its maintenance, but previously the church looked after the graves in the churchyard and those in the graveyard on Londesborough Road.

The following announcement was found in the church records in the Borthwick Institute at York:

THE NEW BURIAL GROUND ON LONDESBOROUGH ROAD.
This was licensed by the Archbishop of York in December 1858 and the first interment took place at the beginning of January 1859.

By order of the church council 26th February 1858 interments must be discontinued forthwith in the parish church of Market Weighton, from and after the first day of January 1859 in the church yard, with the exception of reserved grave space which can be opened without the disturbance of human remains and in which the only bodies to be interred shall be those of the husbands and wives of persons already buried in adjoining graves.

The graveyard on Londesborough Road belonged to the Church and the following appears in Church records:

'The new burial ground was consecrated by Dr. Lonley, Lord Archbishop of York this 12th day of September 1862' signed Joseph Foxley, the vicar at Market Weighton.

The cemetery in Holme Road belongs to the Council and was not opened until 1883. The land was bought from John Proudlock, nurseryman.

In June 1899 the Burial Committee made the following suggestions:

1 That the tool house be painted.
2 The asphalt tarred.
3 The bier be repaired and stained.
4 That steps be taken to prevent the burrowing of rabbits on plots
5 That the five remaining headstones at present standing with the backs to the footpath be turned at the expense of the Council.

From the Council minutes of January 1902:

'The pond to be cleaned out on The Green.
    The grave digger/caretaker for the burial ground, William Moor, left and his brother took his place.
    The grave digger wants a new shovel and pick. He is still having trouble with poultry straying into the cemetery.'

ALLOTMENTS

Another duty of the Council was the provision of allotments, as will be seen by the following entries:

'The following applied for allotments	Acres
Pollard John Jun.	2
Swales John	4
Hall William	4
Cook James	1
Derrick Michael	4
Arnold Joseph	1½
Greenwood George	2
Pollard John Sen.	3
Bell William Jun.	4
Loftus Hugh	4
Chanter Shepherd	4
Haigh Jno.	2
Winter Robert	4
Total	38½ acres

Lord Londesborough has agreed that 14 acres of land for allotments be made into 1-acre plots.'

1913. Preparing for the market at Market Weighton.

Post cart on Northgate, Market Weighton.

MARKET

The market stalls were dealt with by the Council. A meeting held in the Girls' School.

The Clerk read a letter from the Chief Constable giving permission to the shopkeepers of Market Weighton to 'erect stalls in the streets on Saturday from 4 o'clock in the afternoon until 10 o'clock at night provided that no obstruction was caused to footpaths and the free passage of the highway'. On Londesborough Road where the public toilets now are was a brick building owned by the Council in which the market stalls were kept, to be brought out every market day. As this property belonged to the Council it is more than likely the reason they used this small piece of land for the public toilets.

Wednesday was the market day for farmers and market stalls, and Thursday was half-day closing. As far as I can remember, every shop closed.

The cattle market was at the end of Post Office Yard where pens were erected for the purpose.

POSTAL SERVICE

The times given for the post to arrive was remarkably exact considering that it relied on horses, but there must have been times when it was late. In 1823 the post office was in Market Place, the postmaster being James Holmes. A letter sent to Beverley, ten miles away, cost 4d. It would be collected and despatched from Market Weighton at 3.30 am. For letters going to Hull, a matter of 19 miles, the cost would be 5d and collected at the same time, but if going to London (188 miles) the cost would be 11d. for collection at 5.15 pm. The Royal Mail called at the Old King's Arms in High Street at 3.15 am and went to Hull. The only coach service which called at Market Weighton for both Hull and York was Rockingham

Coaches. By 1828 there were two posts a day both to Hull and York. In 1834 the new Royal Mail coaches called at the Devonshire Arms and the Old King's Arms alternatively every morning when it was going to Hull from York but the old Royal Mail coach picked up from the Old King's Arms every night. The journey to York was similar. There were, of course, carriers, possibly about ten or more different individual owners, who would convey other goods coming and going to many places, nearly always using the various inns as a place to collect their goods.

Once the railway came to Market Weighton, goods as well as passengers would go from and to Market Weighton, but the carriers remained in business.

Showing the old Post office.

In the local press, January 1895:

'The postal authorities in Market Weighton during the past week's rough weather had to resort to an improvised sleigh instead of the well known red mail cart to carry mails.'

Allan Johnson said:

'I can remember the post coming like that. They would come from York and change horses at that house on the main road at Barmby Moor and then carry on to Holme. There was a post office opposite the school. I should think he would put his horse in the Blacksmith's Arms.—Sometimes he had to be lifted down because he was so stiff.'

The York post did come that way but much of it also came from Brough.

'MAIL CART ACCIDENT. The following detailed report of the mail-cart smash has been forwarded by an eye-witness. He says Mr. G. Baker, late rulleyman for Mr. Gullick during the last three and a half years, was commencing his duties as mail cart driver, between Market Weighton and Brough, for which Messrs. Conmy Brothers are now the contractors. Mr. A. Conmy was accompanying him to show him the stopping places and his duties generally. The mail cart being very big and uncomfortable for two to ride upon, they decided to use a small wagonette and pair. On reaching South Newbald, a child of about two years of age came running towards the horses. With great presence of mind the driver pulled the horses to the right and succeeded in clearing the child by about three inches, and in so doing the pole broke at the first attempt to pull up the horses, the trap running at their hind quarters, causing the horses to bolt. Both men were thrown off about fifty yards from where the horses first bolted. Baker had his right ankle dislocated and a small bone in the foot fractured. Conmy had his forehead rather badly cut and scrubbed, his nose bruised, and right wrist sprained. Mr. Conmy resumed his journey after having his wounds attended to by Mrs. and Miss Petch. Mr. Petch, farmer, of South Newbald, lent the mail driver his pony and trap, and also kindly undertook to look after the debris in front of his house. Mr. Petch also saw Baker carefully attended to and sent home. The injured men appreciate most heartily the kind treatment they received from Mr., Mrs. and Miss. Petch, and wish, through these columns, to tender their heartfelt thanks to them.'

ELECTRICITY

Bridlington had its own electricity company which was producing power to the town in 1907. Electricity was brought to Market Weighton in September 1933 by Buckrose Light and Power Company based at Driffield. This company was only founded in 1931 and its first shop and offices were at the corner of Lockwood Street and Middle Street South, Driffield. The sub station in Market Weighton is next to the Red Cross hut on Londesborough Road. The overhead line came from Etton and covered Middleton on the Wolds and North Dalton. Pocklington was supplied in the October of the same year. The electricity is thought to have come from Sculcoates power station with an 11,000 watt power line to Driffield. It went from there to Etton. The Buckrose Light and Power Company was bought out on the last day of March 1947 when there were 9,200 customers. The nationalisation into the Yorkshire Electricity Board was on the first day of April 1948, and the records of the Buckrose company are thought to have been destroyed by them. In 1997 it became Yorkshire Electricity Group plc authority and also supplied gas. The church was wired up in 1934 and the Wesleyan chapel in 1937 when the organ there was adapted to play by this means. As mentioned before, the street lights were changed to electricity in 1949 after the nationalisation of gas.

TELEPHONES

Although in 1879 the first public exchange with eight subscribers was available in the City of London, the telephone was not available in Market Weighton until 1910, when ten telephones were allotted to subscribers there.

Number 1 was the public call office at the post office, and then the numbers were allotted to firms and private individuals in alphabetical order. Therefore number 2 was for Dr. Ashwin whose address was given as Beverley Road. Number 3 was Mr. S. T. Cockburn of Holme Road, the hosiery manufacturer, followed by Drake Bros., High Street, drapers and house furnishers. My father's grocer's shop, which was also given as corn merchant, T. G. Lyon & Son, was number 5. Mr. F. J. Masterman, the chemist and druggist next door was 6. The police station was given the number 7. Mr. H. S. Powell, solicitor, Market Place, the founder of the present-day Powell and Young, was number 8. Smith's Tadcaster Brewery was nine, and to ring Mr. T. Todd of Station Road, a cattle dealer, you asked for number 10.

Until 1911 the telephone system was developed by private companies, but, except for Portsmouth and Hull, the Post Office took over the whole of the country in December 1911. In 1910 there were 16 Pocklington subscribers and a further six in 1911, although no more in Market Weighton. Many of these businesses have changed hands in recent years but the solicitors, Powell and Young, have as their number, 872238, and as the number 'eight' was their original number it is one of the few in Market Weighton whose first number still exists.

Telephones in Market Weighton could be used only on weekdays between the hours of 8.30 am and 10 am, the hours when the telephone exchange was manned.

In 1910 the directory urged people to subscribe:

'To be in touch with YOUR FRIENDS, you must have THE TELEPHONE' – 'A necessity of up-to-date business organisation.'

The post office at Market Weighton not only sorted the post and sold stamps, but also had at the rear, the telephone exchange where the switchboard was situated. Before the days of dialling, the receiver was

DON'T DIAL UNTIL "DIALLING" TONE IS HEARD.

Post Office  Telephones.

You can also communicate with :—

FIRE BRIGADE by dialling **5222**

EMERGENCY CALLS (Fire, Police, etc.)

In case of emergency—Dial O and ask operator for the service required.

POLICE   ,,   ,,   **6262**

HOW TO USE THE TELEPHONE.

TO OPERATE THE INSTRUMENT.—

Lift receiver and listen. A continuous low-pitched purring sound (the " dialling " tone) heard in the receiver indicates that dialling may be commenced. When this is heard (**and not before, or the call will be ineffective**), insert finger in hole containing first digit to be dialled, pull dial round to the " stop " and let go, **allowing dial to come to rest before dialling the next digit.** Dial the remaining digits of the required number in the same way. When the called subscriber is being rung, a low-pitched " burr—burr———————burr—burr " (the " ringing " tone) will be heard in the receiver. Allow the "ringing " tone to continue for **at least** half a minute before abandoning the call.

If you hear a high-pitched buzz—buzz—buzz—buzz (the " engaged " tone), indicating that the number dialled or the connecting apparatus is engaged, replace receiver and dial again in about 2 minutes.

If you hear a *continuous* high-pitched buzz (the " number unobtainable " tone) depress receiver rest for **at least** 2 seconds, **listen for " dialling " tone** and carefully re-dial the required number. If the continuous buzz is again heard the number is unobtainable.

If a tone is not heard within half a minute, depress receiver rest for **at least** 2 seconds, **listen for " dialling " tone**, and re-dial the required number.

Errors in dialling. If an error has been made in dialling, depress receiver rest for **at least** 2 seconds, **listen for " dialling " tone**, and dial again.

Do not touch receiver rest except to clear a connection. *Exceptions.*—On calls obtained via **O** the operator may be recalled, if necessary, by moving the receiver rest *slowly* down and up until an answer is received.

Speak clearly, deliberately and directly into the transmitter. Keep earpiece close to ear.

TO ANSWER.—Lift receiver and announce name of subscriber or telephone number.

TO CLEAR.—When conversation is finished, replace receiver **promptly**, earpiece downwards. Unless receiver is on its rest you cannot be called.

TO MAKE CALLS.—In order to ascertain whether the **FULL NUMBER** of the required subscriber or a **SPECIAL CODE NUMBER** should be dialled—*see* notice in your **TELEPHONE DIRECTORY** (which also shows the method of obtaining **TRUNK CALLS**.)

TELEGRAMS.—For Telegram Service (Inland and Foreign) dial **90.**

FAULTS AND ENQUIRIES.—To report faults or make enquiries dial **O.** It may be necessary sometimes to report a fault from another telephone,

Faults may also be reported free of charge from any Call Office.

For information relating to Telegrams, Air Mail, Express, Night Telegraph and Ordinary Letter Services, see over

TE 569   (Farnham)

C 2

(*7358) 34823 2/37 622

Direct Exchange Line (Auto).
Group Service (Auto).
Exchange Line.

All Extensions except Plan 11 Extension No. 1.

[P.T.O.

On right post office, bank, Ladley's garage, Massey's garage and houses beyond, now demolished. Photograph taken in 1960.

The house which was the old police station, and the old fire station next door.

lifted up and the operator at Market Weighton asked what number you required. If the number was local she would connect you, but if you were ringing somebody further away you asked for 'Trunks' and it was passed through to York. The operators were local and one was a relation of my family. If we were out on the Sunday when my sister rang, the operator would ring back later and say, 'Joyce rang earlier.' Another country service!

The telephone exchange on Station Road was built in 1938. In 1999 Kingston Communications of Hull brought their telephone wires to Newbald and Market Weighton after extensive disruption in the town whilst lines were laid under ground.

POLICE AND MAGISTRATES COURT

The first police station of which I am aware was situated on The Green not far from Manor Farm. Within this building was the courtroom. The following article appeared in the press: 'Weighton police station 1901. New building "Under consideration".

'The dawn of the new century has found Market Weighton still in possession of its antiquated, unhealthy and inadequate Police Station! At the last Petty Sessions the Magistrates had a lengthy sitting, which, unfortunately, is not an unusual occurrence – and as the business proceeded the atmosphere became almost unbearable, whilst the walls stream with water. The matter has been under consideration for some time and, at the last meeting of the East Riding Standing Joint Committee, Mr. Powell again raised the question.

A somewhat lengthy discussion ensued, in which Mr. T. N. F. Bardwell is reported to have said that the existing building, in his opinion, was a danger to the Justices and solicitors practising at the Court and even to the prisoners, because it was so damp. His experience was that if he hung his topcoat on the wall it either got wet through or he found the

POCKETS FULL OF SNAILS
(Laughter)

Mr. D. F. Burton said it seemed to the Committee that it would be rather absurd to spend between £4,000 and £5,000 on a new

Police Station at Market Weighton when they had only just built a new Police Station in the same district and only seven or eight miles away – Mr. Powell pointed out that Market Weighton and Pocklington were not in the same district and he contended that there was the same demand for a Court at Market Weighton as at Pocklington, therefore adequate and proper provision should be made – We do hope that the matter will not be tied up with "red tape" and put carefully away in some "pigeon hole".'

It seems from the last statement that things have not changed over the century! However, affairs appear to have progressed as in 1903 a beautiful new Police Station and Court House was opened on Beverley Road and the old one on The Green became the house for the local police sergeant and is now a private house – so presumably the dampness and, hopefully, the snails were dealt with.

In 1917 the twice-monthly sitting was held and the following case was reported:

'Mr. Thomas Bernard Pears was summoned for using an unobscured acetylene lamp on his bicycle. He was fined 5s. and at the same court Mr. Richard Smith of Hull was charged with leaving a motor car on the highway behind the Alma Inn, Market Weighton, without having any lights attached. P.C. Nalton said that on Sunday, December 3rd at 7.30 pm he was on duty in Linegate when he saw a black motor car without lights, at the back entrance to the Alma Inn. Seeing no one in charge he asked for the driver and asked where his lights were. He lit the lamps but they immediately went out as there was no oil in them. He admitted he had not trimmed them that day. A fine of £1 was imposed.'

There were times during the First World War when Market Weighton seemed very law abiding – or there were no policemen to catch them. The following was reported in 1917:

Interior of court house.

'WHITE GLOVES PRESENTED TO THE CHAIRMAN

The magistrates in attendance at the Market Weighton Police Court on Wednesday were Mr. T. G. Lyon, who presided, and Major T. J. Jefferson.

The magistrates' clerk (Mr. T. Robson), as there were no cases down for hearing at the second court in succession, presented a pair of white gloves to the chairman, Mr. Lyon. In doing so he congratulated the Bench, police, and the inhabitants of the Holme Beacon Division on the immunity from crime.

Mr. Lyon, in accepting the gloves, said that the absence of crime in the district was most gratifying; in fact they would have to buy gloves wholesale instead of retail (Laughter). If that state of affairs continued the Petty Sessions, magistrates' clerk and police would have to follow the way of the grand juries. Whilst the golden age was a long way off it was something to make a step towards it. He congratulated the public of Market Weighton and district on their good conduct and hoped when the war was over that the state of affairs would continue satisfactory.'

In December 1995, the magistrates' court on Beverley Road at Market Weighton had been in use for 106 years. It was closed and most petty session cases were transferred to Pocklington. Market Weighton had been the second least used court in the East Riding and averaged about 99 hours of sittings a year. Instead of Market Weighton court, Pocklington was to have almost £10,000 spent on it to bring it up to standard. In December 1999 it was announced that three new court houses would be built. The nearest would be in Beverley and all other courthouses would be closed. At this stage it is not known whether this plan will materialise.

WARTIME SERVICES

During wartime, extra services were needed. The British Red Cross was not a new organisation in the town, but extra people were enrolled and lectures were given in dealing with gas attacks, thankfully never needed. Market Weighton had its own ambulance which was kept in a garage on Londesborough Road (now part of the Red Cross building). It was driven at night by local volunteers and in the day by Alfie Gray. The members of the Red Cross attended the patients on their way to hospital and washed the blankets. Their headquarters and also those of the Air-raid Wardens were in the cottages behind Manor Farm. Mr. Charles Rook who lived there was chief warden and Mrs. Rook was in the Red Cross.

Although Market Weighton had little enemy action, there was still much work for the wardens. When an air-raid was imminent there was a set procedure which had to be carried out. A series of alerts known by different colours showed how close the planes were to our area. The first was a 'yellow' warning which came five to ten minutes before the 'red' warning. This was when the siren sounded. The planes could be bombing five to ten minutes after this. When all the planes had gone and it was safe to come out of the shelter, the 'green' message came through and the 'All clear' siren would be sounded. If, however, the planes went to another area before the 'red alert', there was a 'white' message, which again cleared it. Market Weighton had to alert the wardens in the villages, by telephone, who then went round blowing a loud whistle at the same time as the Market Weighton siren was sounding. Sometimes the siren would not work, and in this case the wardens had to go round the town blowing whistles. This could have been caused by a bird nesting in it. The Home Guard had their headquarters in the Floral Hall. A far greater number of local men joined this, many being local farmers and farm workers who were not called up into the forces. The Women's Voluntary Service (W.V.S.) were on hand to serve food and hot drinks and supply blankets in emergencies and there were volunteers to the Special Constables to assist the police force. The local Fire Brigade has already been described.

Market Weighton branch of the British Red Cross.

'RAILWAYS THROUGH MARKET WEIGHTON – A BRIEF REVIEW'

by John Morfin

The four railway lines to Market Weighton opened as follows to passenger traffic:

From York	4 October 1847
From Selby	1 August 1848
From Beverley	1 May 1865
From Driffield	1 May 1890

Closure of the whole railway presence was effected from 29 November 1965 with the withdrawal of the Hull-Beverley-Market Weighton-Pocklington-York passenger trains.

The principal passenger service for 100 years had provided an alternative rail route for people in Hull and York to travel to the other city rather than through Selby, which with certain short alterations has been available since 1840. The more northern route enabled people in certain Wolds towns and villages to travel quickly to Beverley and Hull, and, to York up to 1965. Express bus services on an often busy major road are now the only public transport available to the residents of Market Weighton, Pocklington etc. to reach the two nearest cities to their homes.

By 1845, the viability of steam locomotive-hauled trains on public railways was well established, and, rapid expansion of the railway system was being promoted and built.

Prominent in several areas of England as a promoter of new railways was George Hudson of York, Chairman of various railway companies including the York & North Midland Railway (Y.&N.M.R.).

Securing the second railway route between Hull and York as well as blocking any competing railway with an ambition to expand into the rich farming area around Market Weighton were strategic objectives of Hudson, whilst providing modern (by mid-19th century standards) goods and passenger facilities for Market Weighton, Pocklington and villages near to the chosen route of a new line from York were obvious benefits to the community and a source of potential revenue.

Initially perceived as a through route from York to Beverley, the first railway to Market Weighton via Stamford Bridge and Pocklington opened to goods and passenger traffic on 4 October 1847. Market Weighton was provided with an imposing passenger station with a small, pillared portico, a roof over the two platforms and two running lines, as designed by the major railway architect, George Townsend Andrews, who designed many splendid structures for new railways promoted by Hudson in the 1840s. Other structures provided initially or soon after opening included the station master's house, the goods shed, the locomotive shed and crossing keepers' cottages.

In 1848, the Selby line was opened, and attractive potential routes for Hudson's competitors to gain access to Hull and East Yorkshire through Market Weighton were occupied by the Y.&N.M.R. Hudson's methods attracted concern and scrutiny, his fall from position of influence was rapid, and, the so called 'Railway Mania' was over in 1849. Thoughts of extending the two railway lines to Market Weighton beyond to connect with the Hull-Bridlington line (also controlled by the Y.&N.M.R.) at Beverley were suspended as investors' confidence in new railway projects was deflated. A period of retrenchment and consolidation in railway management commenced. Thus, by 1850, Market Weighton was the terminus of two railway passenger services from York and from Selby, agricultural produce could travel westwards, but no direct railway communication with Beverley had been built.

An event of major importance to the railways, communities and economy of England north of the Humber and roughly east of the Pennines north of Skipton was the formation of the North Eastern Railway with effect from 31 July 1854, with the Y.&N.M.R. being one of the original constituents.

Until after the First World War, the North Eastern Railway was a vast, profitable, and influential commercial enterprise deriving considerable revenue from an immense mineral traffic in the North East, and to Hull, with substantial revenue from goods and passenger traffic in addition.

Market Weighton eventually achieved more than mere local railway relevance as a centre for its own traffic and that of the immediately surrounding area, when the lines to Beverley and to Driffield were opened in 1865 and 1890 respectively.

The North Eastern Railway operated a Hull-York passenger service from 1865 in addition to the older service via Selby, and created a second route for goods traffic from York and points north to Hull so avoiding the increasingly busy railway junctions at Selby.

The 1890 opening of the Driffield line through the Wolds over Enthorpe Bank generated little local traffic, but enabled the expanding Summer excursion traffic to Bridlington and Filey from the West Riding and beyond to be routed more directly than through the congested railway system in Hull. Thus, Market Weighton found itself as a junction of two significant, if secondary, lines from 1890, and through trains shared the tracks with, for example, local passenger trains calling at all stations to Selby, and pick up trains between Hull and York.

Development of motor transport from the 1920s, particularly bus services able to travel through the centre of villages, and lorries capable of being driven into farms gradually depleted railway revenues, with Market Weighton's circumstances being typical of hundreds of other places.

Local passenger trains calling at small stations on the Selby and Driffield lines were withdrawn after 18 September 1954, and Fangfoss and Warthill stations on the York line lost their passenger services on 3 January 1959. Goods traffic by rail to village and country town stations declined continuously in the 1950s, and June 1965 was the last month of goods traffic at remaining small stations on the lines to Beverley and York, except Pocklington and Market Weighton. The era of 'Beeching Cuts' was now decimating railway facilities and services around Britain, and the last day of operations at Market Weighton was on 27 November 1965 with the last York–Beverley–Hull passenger train hauled by the now preserved steam locomotive 61306.

Agricultural traffic was moved entirely by motor lorry, private car ownership continued to rise, British Rail virtually abandoned the marketing of holiday and excursion traffic to the seaside including Bridlington, and the positive impression of the formerly busy railway presence at Market Weighton has receded into distant memory.

After 1965 the railway fabric in Market Weighton deteriorated quite rapidly after the removal of the permanent way. The attractive station building had its roof removed in 1947, but, by 1978, the structure was derelict with one of the portico pillars cracked. The locomotive shed which had been closed as a First World War economy measure survived as a reminder of a country railway junction of some importance. Devoid of its roof, the Andrews-designed passenger station had not warranted statutory listing as a building of special architectural and historic interest by 1978 so it was a likely candidate for demolition, which was effected that year. Housing has obliterated much of the site of the former railway presence in Market Weighton, and the built environment is much the poorer for the loss of the station, formerly one of the noteworthy buildings in the town.

Demolishing the station.

The signal box demolished.

NEWS OF THE RAILWAY

The first train travelled the 21 miles from York in 1847. The newspaper of the day reported the occasion:

'A numerous and respectable party of gentlemen celebrated this important event by dining at the Devonshire Arms Hotel, Market Weighton (Londesborough Arms), having had an excursion from York. There was champagne, food piled high on the tables and speeches from important people.'

Another excursion in 1928 was far from pleasant:

'An alarming experience befell over a hundred local residents who, after spending Whit Monday at Bridlington, left by train for home. The train proceeded rather slowly until it approached Market Weighton when the engine appeared to gather speed down an incline until the train rushed at full speed through Market Weighton station creating consternation among the local passengers. The train proceeded at full speed and passed through Pocklington station without stopping. One of the excursionists, a local postman, who was expected on duty early in the morning, at once brought the train to a stop about half a mile through Pocklington by pulling the communication cord, for which act the other passengers felt indebted. After being detrained at Pocklington station they were conveyed in three motor buses to Market Weighton, arriving home about one o'clock in the morning.

Many of the victims desire to express their appreciation of the kindness displayed by the Pocklington station master in getting the stranded passengers conveyed to their homes.'

Digging the Driffield line near Market Weighton.

Digging the Driffield line near Market Weighton.

Collecting wood from station.

Inside the station, before 1935.

Market Weighton station from Londesborough Road, before 1939.

The station from the church tower, about 1930.

One of the last trains from Hull.

Model of Market Weighton station, made by Malcolm Baker.

A WALK DOWN THE MAIN STREET

In order to look at the main street of Market Weighton as it is, and as it was, we will stroll from Northgate, or, as it is now, York Road, and come on to the area which was the Market Hill. To the right you would have seen the Alma Inn and other houses. I cannot remember the inn. There was the pump on the part of the Market Hill which now is the road from Holme Road. Where there were houses is now the bus shelter, and gardens. This scheme was voted the winner from eleven entries in the new building section of East Yorkshire Borough Council's design awards scheme for 1994. The building of the shelter was a controversial subject, because of its high cost. The idea was to improve the look of the town, which it has.

Where the market is held in 2000 there were cottages and, during the war, a very big tank of water for Fire Brigade emergencies. What of the future? The matter is under negotiation and next year we may see new council offices or a town hall. It will not be the first time that this idea has emerged. In 1897, just over a hundred years ago, the following report was given to the Council by the Public Hall Committee, and on land near to the site which is now under consideration.

'After carefully considering the question of a site for the proposed Public Hall your committee are of the opinion that the best site for the purpose, which is available is one situate in Northgate adjoining the Congregational Church and belonging to Mrs. Elizabeth Gibson. This will afford ample room for a good hall with ante rooms and a Caretaker's Cottage, and leave plenty of room for accommodation necessary for the Fire Engine and its equipment. It also has the advantage of having two entrances. One on Northgate and one on the Londesborough Road and a privileged footpath could be formed which would be a great convenience to residents in and about Northgate, in going to and from the station.

'Mrs. Gibson is agreeable to sell the property for £150 and the Committee consider this a reasonable price and recommend the Council to sanction a provisional agreement being entered into with Mrs. Gibson to purchase the property if the scheme is sanctioned by the authorities. The Committee also suggest that the Council empower them to take all the necessary steps required to prepare the scheme for the County Council and the Local Government Board and that they quote the sum of £1,250 as the maximum sum that will be required. Signed by J. W. Hollings, Chairman of the Committee.'

The Committee wanted to borrow the sum of £1,600 for the purpose of the buildings suggested by the report, but the Local Government Board said that this loan had been refused by the County Council of the East Riding of Yorkshire, and, therefore, no hall was built. When Mrs. Gibson's thatched cottages were demolished a new row of brick-built cottages was built instead and is still there today, as the report indicated, 'adjoining the Congregational Church', or as it is now, the Sports and Camping shop.

It seemed appropriate to quote this report in detail as at the time of writing Market Weighton Town Council is

Northgate showing the Congregational Church and the thatched cottage where the town hall was to be built.

Market day on a summer Saturday in 1905.

Interior of Congregational Church

Northgate looking to Market Hill.

Hydes Gauling (now demolished), near the market.

negotiating what I imagine will be a much smaller building at a far greater cost.

From this point we make our way along Market Place to a shop next to the market. At the moment empty, it has been The Chocolate Box and a shop selling tackle for ponies and their riders, but was, earlier, a shoe shop, firstly owned by Mr. Duffield and then Charles Ullyott. Before the new Lloyds Bank was built there was an archway through to Hydes Gauling. This my family called Duffield's Yard for obvious reasons. In it were about six cottages, two being of one storey. This yard came out on to Londesborough Road. On the other side of the archway was a shop belonging to Dickinson Consitt whose firm, according to his advertisement, were, 'Joiners, cabinet makers, upholsterers, painters, paper hangers, house furnishers and undertakers'. His workshops were in Chapel Yard where the Wesleyan Chapel hall stands in 1999.

Lloyds Bank used the shop premises until, in 1960, it erected on the same site a bigger building. This is of a traditional character, constructed of load-bearing walls and part steel frame, to avoid columns inside the bank. The external elevation facing the Market Hill is of a Georgian character, faced with local handmade bricks and some Portland stone. All the doors and windows facing the front are in polished mahogany, as are the main

Mr. Consitt's workmen with their tools.

Mr. Consitt's work shop down Chapel yard, now Chapel hall.
D. Consitt, A. Kneeshaw, W. Moore,
R. Langrick, S. Hornsey, N. Dixon, S. Mizon.

fittings inside the bank. The part of the old building above the archway was not renewed, so eliminating this old feature.

Part of Lloyds Bank is on the site of another shop which was a saddler's. This belonged to George Priestman, and before this Mr. S. A. Haddon and Son.

The Griffin public house is one of the oldest inns in Market Weighton and was certainly there before 1823. To the right is another archway.

A shop which has stood empty for some years, since Loft's electrical shop closed, was in old photographs called 'Cordingley', a drapery firm from Hull and Beverley. Charles Stather moved in next and was there until he retired. He also had a draper's shop in Pocklington.

The next two houses have sometimes been shops and at other times private houses, but the next shop has been a stationer's since before 1867 when William Wilson owned it. I remember it belonging to his son, Percy Wilson; according to his advertisement, he sold useful presents. His slogan was 'Just the thing you want at Just the price you want to pay'. He also sold novels, magazines and news-papers, was sole agent for Goss and Crest china, leather goods, toys, games and music. In the back of the shop was a lending library. He was also a printer, and works at the rear of the shop are still being used for this purpose. In 1867, William Wilson published the *Yorkshireman's News* every Wednesday. The stationer's was not always the end building. The house next to it was a substantial private house. Older local people say that it belonged to Mr. Holmes. This house was demolished to widen Londes-borough Road, which must have been very narrow before.

Walk carefully across the road as the traffic is quite heavy, although much better since the bypass was built. On a summer Sunday evening when the railway station was still in use, there could be queues of cars as far back as the Londesborough crossroads. This queue was caused by excursions, particularly on Bank Holidays, when the trains were so long that they had to pull up twice to allow passengers to alight on to the platform. An R.A.C. officer

Market Hill, late thirties. Mr. Consitt's shop is on the right.

A band on the Market Hill, 1905.

Holme Road.

Holme Road, about 1944.

Market Place.

*Mr. Sanderson outside
Robinson's chemist's shop.*

Mrs. Barnes' oven.

would be on point duty to help the traffic out on to the street. Most of the traffic would go along Holme Road, back to the West Riding. There was no bypass across the York Road at Shiptonthorpe then, so all cars from the Bridlington road came through Market Weighton. The main street was not given back to the people of Market Weighton until the Hull to York bypass was opened in March 1991 by David Davis M.P.

All the following properties have no particular history except that they are thought to be the result of stall holders wanting more stable businesses. One property was an inn called the White Swan, known locally as the Mucky Duck.

Harry Potter's shop, which I have already described when I looked back to my childhood, came next, and then a shop which was the premises of three different chemists: Charles Robinson's, Richard Johnson's and Selles before both they and Mr. Richard Johnson moved across the road. Mr. Robinson was the sole agent for Rexall products and advertised that there was 'a Rexall Product for every common ailment and a Rexall Toilet Requisite for every need'.

Three shops from the end of the Market Place is a property with a lovely oak bow window, though it has for some years been painted. It was put in by Mr. Arnett of Beverley, but in the 1920s and 30s it belonged to Mr. and Mrs. George Barnes. The kitchens were in the basement, and, as in all these premises, were below grave level in the churchyard behind. In Mrs. Barnes' kitchen was a large baking oven. She was a very good cook and made all the things for sale in the shop and also provided dinners for farmers on Market Day. The farmers ate their dinner at one end of the basement and I have been told that Mrs. Barnes laid a table at the back of the shop too. These dinners would be cheaper than those at the Londesborough Arms. Their advertisement didn't mention these dinners, but that could have been in earlier years:

'George Barnes
Temperance Refreshment House. Grocer, Confectioner and Provision Dealer.
Caterers for Teas and Cyclists
Try our home-made bread. Speciality: Carrs Malt Bread.'

Next to Ladley's, where 'farmyard' was sold in 1930, was a boot and shoe shop under the name of Robert Layton. In many old photographs the name can be seen on the end, but in one of 1906 he advertised himself as a picture framer with a Registry Office for Servants.

In 1899 November Market Weighton Hirings were reported in the newspaper:

'These hirings were held in beautiful weather. There was only a small attendance and engagements were few. Foremen were asking £22-£30, waggoners £17-£20 and second -class ploughmen £16-£17.' These wages were, of course, for a year.

Market Place, about 1906, showing the old chemist's shop on the left.

Londesborough Arms, 1904.

Les Layton painting Walter Willson's old shop.

George Parkinson and his daughter Nellie.

The hirings took place outside the Londesborough Arms, which comes next and marks the beginning of High Street. It was built as a coaching and posting inn by the 5th Duke of Devonshire. Soon after 1800 he called his inn the New Royal Arms to distinguish it from the Old Royal Arms. The name was changed to the Devonshire Arms until 1850, when the Lordship of the Manor moved from the Duke of Devonshire to Lord Londesborough, and its name changed again to the Londesborough Arms. For very many years it was in the ownership of only two families, the Simpson's and the Bell's. It was a country hotel which served as the centre of the corn market and a meeting place for farmers on market day. It still has the coiled serpent from the Cavendish Arms carved in the original stone headpiece of the fire surround in the Devonshire Room. It was completely refurbished, having been closed for about a year, and re-opened in February 1991 with 15 bedrooms. It has had a chequered life since the stability of the many years under the Simpson's and Bell's but was voted Hotel of the Year in the annual Yorkshire and Humberside Tourist Board's White Rose Award in September 1991.

Part of the hotel which is now a coffee lounge was the shop belonging to Walter Willson of Newcastle but for many years before this was another grocer's shop, belonging to Austin Gullick and his wife. The shop beyond this belonged to the Parkinson family. It was said to be a drapery and grocery store.

Among the many goods which George Parkinson had for sale were 'Witney' blankets, crib and coloured blankets, quilts in coloured wool, Alhambra, scarlet Worsted etc. White toilet quilts, eiderdown quilts, and white and coloured toilet covers'. He sold Irish linen sheeting, white and unbleached twilled cotton, seamless pillow calico and ticks. Feather beds, bolsters and pillows were made at short notice. Corsets were sold with a wide variety of makes, for example, 'Cestus', 'Guaranteed', 'Phyllis', 'Diagonal Seam' and several other well-known makes, as well as 'Tendimus self-fitting elastic skirt bands'. He was also an agent for the new straight-needled sewing machine from Wheeler and Wilson. It was amazing because 'it would stitch 3,000 stitches a minute, and perfection because it was noiseless and was the fastest and easiest running machine in the world with a spool which held 100 yards of cotton'. A billhead in 1872 stated that he was a family grocer and tea dealer, linen and woollen draper, silk mercer and haberdasher, selling also for family mourning and furnishing funerals. The bill was for a felt hat, so that must have been another line. Many other shops sold a great variety of different products, mixing drapery, groceries and hardware.

Late night opening is not a new idea, for George Parkinson and most shops were open until 7 pm, with opening until 8 pm on Wednesday market day, and 10 pm each Saturday.

These premises were for many years the shop and office for the *Hull Daily Mail*. In 1999 it is a pet shop. Mr. Parkinson and his family lived in the house above and at the back of the shop, with their garden to its right, with high iron railings at the front. It was eventually sold and a small butcher's shop erected on it. It belonged to Harry Walker who we knew as 'Butcher Walker', as there were other Walker's, in business in the town. It has since been a café and shop known as The Buttered Bun, opened by Mrs. Jackson, whose family also delivered milk from Pocklington and Market Weighton.

The next premises, which have only recently been altered, is a bakery shop belonging to the Scarborough firm of Coupland's, but was, at one time, the Yorkshire Penny Bank. In 1937 and before, the same bank was open in the school on Hungate (Spring Road) each Monday from 6.30 to 7.30 pm. In the adjoining property on High Street was a school, which my mother attended. It was at one time a café run by Mrs. Bastiman,

Horse fair.

High Street, 1913.

68

The Celebrated Trotter

MERRY LEGS,

THE PROPERTY OF

Mr. William Brigham, of Market-Weighton,

WILL SERVE MARES THIS SEASON, 1834,

At One Pound Fourteen Shillings each Mare.

MERRY LEGS was got by Mr. Robert Ramsdale's Performer, or Mr. Kirby's Lottery. Merry Legs is four years old, a Dark Chestnut, stands 15 hands and 2 inches high; his dam by Sportsman the Celebrated Mare of Mr. Lund of Bielby, one of first Rate Hackneys, which trotted a mile within 3 minutes different times. Sportsman, was bred by Captain Earle, of Benebrough Hall, Sportsman's dam was nearly thoroughbred, which trotted Nine Miles in half an hour, at different times, between Benebrough and York. Merry Legs is own brother to the Celebrated Black Mare, bred by Mr. Lund, and performed a distance of one Hundred Miles, in Eleven Hours and 18 Minutes, when only two Years old.

Merry Legs is Brother to the Chestnut Horse, that trotted when four Years old, two Miles in six Minutes and 27 Seconds, and was Sold for £110, also to the Bay Horse, that trotted in June 1830, Seventeen Miles within the Hour, trotting his last Mile and a half in four Minutes. In August 1830, he beat Mr. Hutchinson's Brown Horse at Doncaster, for £50 each, four Miles, trotting it in Eleven minutes and 45 Seconds each. In February 1831 he was matched to Trot Eighteen Miles within the hour, and lost by bieng too tight in his breast girth, and only went Seventeen Miles and a Quarter, carrying Ten Stones and a Half, and the day after was refused £250 from His Grace the Duke of Gordon, and afterwards Sold to him in London, on the 21st. of April.

Merry Legs is Descended from the first Blood, and the fastest Trotters in the Kingdom, the Proprietor challenges him to Walk, Trot, and Gallop, any Covering Stallion in Yorkshire.

N.-B. He will be shown at Market Weighton, Howden, Selby, York, and Pocklington, and will Travel their Respective Neighbourhoods.

The Money to be paid at Midsummer to the Groom, for which he is Accountable.
J. Crabtree, Printer, and Book-Binder, Market Weighton.

Robert Ramsdale, a horse dealer, was at the Old King's Arms.

and has also been a variety of other businesses. One of these two houses was the centre for distributing gas masks in 1939. According to William Watson's 1848 map, this is where William Boast had his business and sold the Market Weighton maps.

Next on the map was a large inn called the Old King's Arms owned and licensed by Robert Ramsdale. He is shown as the proprietor in 1823, when the inn was the Excise office. The family, which included Thomas Ramsdale, were horse dealers from Holme on Spalding Moor. The Old King's Arms seems to be in existence until about 1864 when it must have been demolished. A three-storey building replaced it where Birch's electrical shop is now.

The next building is an old property belonging to the church. The first house was the home and business of 'Plumber Watson', and strangely in the old 1848 map was also lived in by a plumber and glazier, Henry Low. In the same block is a business which the old people will call 'Reasbeck's' and those a little younger will call 'Hatfield's', but in both cases was a tailor's.

Reasbeck and Son described themselves as 'Ladies' and Gentlemen's Tailors and Breeches Makers' They claimed to offer reasonable prices and first class workmanship. Hugh Hatfield had a very similar trade. This shop still sells clothes but for females only.

A small shop next to the tailor's belonged, first of all, to Mr. Walter Gilson, who was a watch and clock maker, and later to his daughter, Miss Alice Marion Gilson, who was not young and always served the watches and jewellery wearing a hat and often a woolly scarf round her neck. She must have learnt the trade from her father.

Bogg's wet fish shop came next. It was run by the Bogg family for many years. Wonderful fresh fish was brought by their own lorry from the pier at Bridlington, where they landed their own fish.

The next shop was one which all children remembered, Kitty Vause's sweet shop, now very different because it is a modern boutique. Kitty Vause ran a shop which not only satisfied her little customers but Kitty as well.

Two small cottages come next. They are little changed from the years gone by. Alwyn Davis's father, having worked as a baker at Kemp's, started a little bakery in one of the cottages where he lived. The other belonged to Miss King, a draper. Strange to say, both shops still bear a certain resemblance to their past trade.

My uncle was next: George Newbury had a butcher's shop where Hagston's butcher's is now. My uncle and aunt and their two children lived in the house at the side and above and slaughtered the animals in the building behind the shop. These buildings now sell car accessories. After this was a shoe shop, and then Mrs. Bird's shop, a little confectioner's.

After the entrance to The Arch was the cinema already discussed. The Red Lion and Finkle Street end the north side of the main street and we cross over to the other side of the road where there is now a row of shops and a restaurant. This was Robert B. Massey's car show room with petrol pumps. Behind this were the workshops where Rolls Royce cars and others were repaired. This building was not there before the war and started up in the name of Massey and Pepper Co. Mr. Pepper was an electrician in Hull and wired up much of Market Weighton in the early days of electricity. They also started the garage at Woodside on the Bridlington Road.

Before Massey's building in High Street was built, there were houses and premises owned by John Ernest Brown, mineral water manufacturer and ale and

Charabanc in Finkle Street.

porter merchant and bottler. When larger factories started up he emigrated to Canada. His two sisters, Annie and Alice Brown, stayed in Market Weighton living on Beverley Road. There was also the King's Head public house, which was demolished. In 1809 it was let to a Robert Bland and included brewing equipment so it must have brewed its own beer at that time.

The next important building was the Primitive Methodist chapel, but it was not the first, nor even the second of this name. The first was a very small building built before 1848 on the right of Beverley Road, but as the congregation grew it became far too small, and so it was demolished and a second one built in 1860 on its site. This building is still there and, although altered and painted, the original chapel windows can still be seen. This also became too small, so another much more decorative building was erected in 1902 on the site of the old Temperance Hall, which had been built in 1841. The hall was intended to be used for concerts, lectures, readings and other 'respectable' entertainment. There is little to discuss about its 62-years' life except a programme for a concert given on a Tuesday evening in January 1877. This was announced as a 'GRAND CONCERT given by York Minster Quartette. The artists included Mr. J. E. Wilkinson – alto, Messrs. T. Baines and J. Humphries – tenors and Mr. A. McCall – basso'. Tickets could be reserved for two shillings, Second seats for one shilling to be obtained from Mr Hunter, Schoolmaster or Mr. Wilson, Post Office. The doors opened at 7 pm and the concert commenced at 7.30 pm. Its life came to an end and the Primitive Methodists bought it, knocked it down and built the property which is still there, although its use has changed. The chapel was opened in August 1902:

'The opening of the twentieth century has been rendered memorable to local Primitive Methodists by the erection of a new church at Market Weighton. The Society has laboured in the town for upwards of fifty years and the present undertaking may be taken as indicative of the vigorous life and buoyant enterprise of local Primitive Methodism, for, to quote the words used by the Rev. James Pickett at the foundation stone laying of the new building – "one can hardly imagine a declining church with vitality enough in it to face the responsibility of bricks and mortar to the tune of many hundreds of pounds". The premises erected on Beverley Road in 1860 have long been inadequate to the needs of the Society, and every department of their work was so seriously hindered that a more commodious and suitable building was an imperative necessity. Last year a scheme for the erection of the new church was projected and the appeal for funds was so liberally responded to that in October the foundation stones were "well and truly" laid.'

'The building which consists of church and school premises has been reared in the principal thoroughfare on the site of the old Temperance Hall and in every way is admirably calculated to serve the purposes for which it is intended. It has a frontage of 34 feet and its erection has effected an architectural improvement to the street. The structure is of red brick with stone dressings and all the internal woodwork is of pitch pine. Seating accommodation is provided for 230, all pews being on the ground floor, with raised platform for the choir. The architect is Mr. W. G. Smithson of Leeds. A valuable American organ has been presented to the trustees by Messrs. G. Barnes, S. T. Cockburn and Mr. W. Walmsley. The estimated cost of the building, including the site, is £1,000.'

This was the second Primitive Chapel, Beverley Road, on the site of the first one.

The Primitive Chapel in High Street, with the old Temperance Hotel to the right.

The church continued enjoying a good congreg[ation]
until after the First World War when, as in many
churches, numbers began to dwindle. In 192[?]
began between the Primitive and We[sleyan]
Methodists and in 1934 a common circuit of
branches was started. In 1947 the two
Weighton churches amalgamated. Mornin[g]
were held in St. John's Wesleyan chapel wi[th]
services in the Primitive Methodist chu[rch ...]
1955 all the services were held at St. Joh[n's].

There was now no reason to keep the [?]
as it was a substantially built propert[y]
and became a grocer's shop belonging t[o ?]
who had, with her mother, Mrs. Mi[?]
business at the corner shop in Saint [?]
for many years. Later the old chapel [?]
Centre and in 1999 is a Fitness Cer[tre ?]
a popular place for the people of th[e ?]
energy now that vacuum cleaners,[?]
and cars leave the population in ne[ed ?]
for their energy! There have be[en ?]
types of use for this one site.

Next door was the Tempera[nce ?]
in 1848 by John Shields but [?]
same year it was called a Tem[perance ?]
Ann Shields, the wife of John [?]
Hotel in 1865 aged 76 and [?]
just over two years more. H[?]
buried in the Londesborou[gh ?]

In 1855 James Merkin [?]
makers and agricultural [?]
founders, timber mercha[nts ?]
owners, in the land behi[nd ?]
firm was called Merkin B[?]
taken a partner, as it [?]
Tomkins and, as wel[l ?]
agricultural engineers [?]
they were wheelwright[s ?]
Harry Eglin took over [?]
Mr. Eglin lived on Bev[erley ?]
Street was another ag[?]
brass and iron foun[dry ?]
William Steel, who a[?]
News 1867.

The firm of Ladley and Son had star[ted as ?]
engineers in the front part of the old Temperan[ce]
property. Ladley's were in these premises for many years.
They had petrol pumps on the raised step in front of the
house. In order to be used, the hose had to be slung
across the pavement above the heads of passers by. This
eventually had to be discontinued. In 1999 there is no
petrol station in the town. There is still a motor engineer
in the same premises, Frank Scaife.

The Hull Banking Company came to Market
Weighton in 1838 when it opened an agency, but the
name of Midland Bank was first seen in 1901. It was
the result of mergers. The bank agency may have been
in a building on that site. The present building was
not there in 1848 and it is thought that the same
architect who designed the brewery could have also
designed this and the building which is now the post
office, in about 1887. The bank is still in the same
building but had a major refurbishment in 1995. It
acquired two new interview rooms and a larger
banking hall and now has a cash machine installed.
The main difference will be the added security which,
unfortunately, has become necessary in all places
where money, is handled.

[P]ost Office, belonged
[? wine] and spirit merchant.
[? Per]cy's dram shop'. It
[? when i]t moved from Market
[? bu]ilding is known as Post
[? was] Prospect Row. These
[? s]ome years ago. In their
[? no]w belonging to the Elgey
[? ...] the Scout hut and the

[? ther]e were the sheep and cattle
[? It i]s strange to think today that
[? Wo]rld War sheep and cattle were
[? alon]g the roads and streets. I
[?] Walter Newbury, driving them
[?] Londesborough Road, up to
[?] with one person walking ahead
[? g]arden gates. I am told that when
[?]igham moved from The Chestnuts,
[? in 189]9, the sheep, at least, were driven
[?] House Farm up the Beverley Road
[? to Shi]pton, but spent a night resting at
[?] at Shipton.

[? bac]k on to the street and following our
[?], we reach a shop which was built by
[? ...]ley. It has been used for a variety of
[? In] 1848 it was a very small building, the
[?] Inn. The next property, all now belonging
[? ...]s auctioneers and estate agents, was once
[?]s, Mrs. Jackson's café and shop and
[?]s electrical shop. Stanley Adamson was a
[?] and electrician. In old photographs taken
[? 19]05 the property on High Street had a very
[?] finish. It belonged to a painter and decorator
[?] Bates Wadsworth, who was obviously
[? advert]ising his expertise by having 'trompe-d'oeil'
[? paint]ed brickwork. Before this the building was just
[? lim]ewashed, as it was afterwards.

[? B]arclays Bank is next. It was built in 1897 in the
[? En]glish Renaissance style', the architects being Penty
[? an]d Penty of York. The two houses shown on the 1848
[? m]ap were obviously demolished in order to build this
[? v]ery substantial and elegant building. In the old
[?] houses, was a surgeon or general practitioner,
Matthew Jackson, who later lived at Ashfield on
Londesborough Road. In 1848 the other house was
occupied by James Holmes, the post master, so
presumably this would be another building which has
been used as a post office.

A typical old coaching inn comes next, the Half
Moon with its archway to a yard behind. One can
visualise a farmer leading his horse and trap and
disappearing through into it. A small room on the
other side of the arch was where, certainly in Victorian
times, the ladies waited for their farmer husbands to
– eventually – come out of the inn. The extra clothes
which they wore on the cold ride home would, no
doubt, be welcome in that little room as there would
be no heater to keep them warm and some of the
farmers would, I am sure, stay longer than they said
they would, talking and drinking. William Jewison,
who at one time owned the Half Moon, held the rights
for the Trafalgar stage coach which operated between
Hull and York.

I can remember when, in about 1958, Mr. and Mrs.
Smithies, who were at the Blacksmith's Arms (now
the Chinese Restaurant) in Shipton, brought the beer
and other drinks from the kitchen in a jug and the

The old Primitive Methodist Chapel, about 1997.

Merkin and Tomkins.

Looking east from Church tower, 1997, on Giant Bradley day.

The back of Providence Row, about 1931.

High Street, showing the building with its walls painted, 1905.

customers sat on high-backed wooden settles in the front room. It was not only called the Blacksmith's Arms: Mr. Smithies was a working blacksmith, which his name implied.

Another very old building comes next, now in Market Place. I have been told that it is one of the oldest properties still standing in the town. Its frontage has been altered dramatically as, when it belonged to Mr. Masterman, and even when Mr. Johnson moved in, it still had a very old bow window. Inside were all the little wooden drawers and cupboards which must have been there a very long time. The window and door are now in the Castle Museum in York and, I expect, in the old street scene. Selles Chemists put modern shop windows into the old house and shop, now including the ladies' tailor's shop run for many years by Edith Kelsey (Davis). Here many Weighton girls learnt the skills of dressmaking and tailoring. It was just outside this building that the concrete road barrier was built during the Second World War.

Dentist in 1996.

I will say no more about the next building as I have already said enough except to add that it too is a very old building which has been altered so many times, not only by my ancestors but in more recent times. The old hand-made bricks on the wall facing Selles Chemists reveal all. The chemist's yard is, in 1999, still the way to the Council offices, situated in the bedrooms of the old house. The dentist's surgery was also up those funny old stairs but now occupies one of the outbuildings where Selles kept empty boxes until they were burnt. It has been beautifully restored.

In nearly all these yards, cottages were built. Many have been demolished whilst others were turned into warehouses.

Having passed by my own family's business quickly, we come to the large Victorian building beyond, built in about 1878. The old building was built some time before 1761. It was two buildings, the first one a house and the second, after 1822, a public house, the Cross Keys. A relic of the old building can still be seen on the

wall facing down the street. It is, I am told by Bruce Miles, a thick chalk wall with an old hand-made brick covering. It seems that the new building was built after the demolition of the old one. In 1873 the Cross Keys was unoccupied and it may be that it was then decided to demolish it. John Everingham, a draper and tailor, had just bought it from the executors of Robert Laister.

In 1879 the new building was described as a:

'messuage with appurtenances in Highgate, Market Place, Market Weighton, recently pulled down and two modern houses with shops, in occupation of Messieurs Everingham and Son, clothier and outfitter, and Mr. William Jones, erected on the site.'

In 1889 the shop was leased to Thomas Johnson Galland, a draper of Market Weighton, with a workshop, warehouse, joint use of the yard and part of the garden. His son, Arthur Thomas Galland, who by this time owned the property, had left for America in 1885 and died intestate in Cartagena, Columbia, in 1894. His father, being the heir, then became the owner until 1910 when he was 86 and had carried on business in the town for 50 years. He sold to Samuel Cooper with Henry Duffield, boot and shoe maker, in the other.

Samuel Cooper was the son of Job Cooper, a veterinary surgeon and churchwarden in Market Weighton. Job died in 1873 aged only 42, leaving a big family. The ironmonger's business was carried on by Samuel Cooper's son and son-in-law, and later his grandson, Bruce Miles, who incorporated both properties into one big shop and continued there until his retirement in 1986 when two shops were made once more.

The second shop in this block, which had been the Cross Keys Inn, still has the old cellars of the inn. In the shop was a draper, Charles

Market Place, site of Cross Keys Inn.

Maurice Cooper and Wilfred Miles outside their shop.

Rickatson's shop, now Dyson's, jewellers.

Stather, cousin to Samuel Cooper. He later moved to the shop which had belonged to Cordingley's. Fowler's were the next drapers to follow Stather's

This next property is one of the older ones in Market Weighton, but the first information is from about 1848 when Thomas Nornabell owned the property. He was not married and when he died in 1907 he left it to his niece, Annie Inglis, who was the daughter of his sister and wife of James Brown Inglis. He was a watchmaker and jeweller at 4 Coney Street in York. The family is still in business in York today.

In 1885 Alfred Rickatson started up in business as a clothier, outfitter and boot dealer. His son, George Rickatson, continued after his father's death in 1934 and also gave a service which was usual in those days. He travelled to houses and farms regularly with samples of clothing and boots, and delivered them the next week, using a motor cycle and sidecar and later a Singer car from 1930. For example, Monday was the day to travel round Holme on Spalding Moor, and Friday was the day for Hotham and Newbald. In the Newbald area were four houses which amongst them had 48 children. The Rickatson children were expected to give them some of their toys. Sacks of apples grown on the many apple trees in the Rickatson's long garden were also gathered up and taken to them. Down the yard is an old mail coach shed and Francis Hydes' old blacksmith's shop. I also remember Mr. Hobson mending shoes in one of the old cottages after the war.

In the next yard was the veterinary surgery, first belonging to Mr. Hickes and then to Mr. J. P. Cook, who worked for him. Mr. Cook moved into the house in the yard in 1931 when he married, and by that time, 1926, Mr. Hickes had built Givendale Lodge on land belonging to Manor Farm on Spring Road. In 1937 the surgery was moved to Londesborough Road, where Mr. Cook had built a house. The shop at the front was a draper's owned by Mrs. Crumpton, but she was in business there as Winifred Kelsey before her marriage. Upstairs was a hairdresser's. An advertisement stated:

> 'Charm lies not alone in appearance but in the quality of the material. Winifred Kelsey can offer her patrons the highest quality and the most reasonable prices in millinery, jumpers, frocks, children's underwear, art silk and wools and all ladies' wear.'

This building, and the next, which is an accountant's, were both built at the same time and could have been one large house belonging at one time to George Scott, a corn miller.

Further down the street towards the Market Hill is a shop which seems to have been associated with food for a long time. The present-day property was

Market Place, about 1920, from Church tower.

not there in 1848 and the old chapel was not approached through an arch. The shop is on the left of the archway.

A story which my uncle told has been verified: John Creamer was a baker there in the late 1800s. He was known locally as Johnny Creamer. I have been told that one day he left a note saying: 'Int' tank.' They found that the poor man had committed suicide by drowning in a water tank outside the back door of his bakery. He was still there according to the 1893 directory, but not that of 1901, and I have found no further mention of the family since then, in spite of his being part of a large family. Thomas was also a baker in Market Place, and another property in High Street belonged to his son, Thomas Hessell Creamer, also a baker.

When Johnny Creamer died the property was sold to Mr. J. B. Kemp and Son and was still a bakery. I have an old postcard which showed this shop. On it, somebody had written 'Penny Bun'. I have been told people could go there and buy a big iced bun for one penny. Mr. Kemp senior died in 1926 and his son, Arnold Kemp, the father of Jean Kemp, continued in business until 1934 when the premises was bought by Hull and East Riding Co-operative Society, which ran it as a café. It then became a confectioner's belonging to Mrs. Ward and was called The Tuck Shop. It is now a Chinese Take Away.

The chapels have already been discussed.

There is just one small street which we have not visited. This is Linegate. Where Powell and Young's car park has been made was a yard called Garden Place, a very beautiful sounding name. Unfortunately the houses there were not as inspiring as the name. Garden Place was eventually demolished.

These yards throughout the town housed many families. Their children often grew up in very primitive conditions but they are now the backbone of the older members of the population of Market Weighton and district. Modern parents would not accept those conditions and the people who are deciding to live away from large towns and join the Market Weighton community also want larger and more convenient housing.

In 1999 the following estates have been given planning permission: on Beverley Road 129 properties, 214 between Cliffe Road and Hawling Road, 52 between Cliffe Road and Sancton Road, and other smaller estates. Six classrooms are being built at the infants' school, some to replace the 'prefabs'. How different this is from the end of the 19th and early 20th century, when the town was in decline and no houses were being built.

Until the 2001 census it will not be possible to say exactly how many people live here but it is certainly more than it has ever been. As a result, the shops are also beginning to come back to life.

We are now back from our walk along the main street and have arrived at the

Market Hill, where all the buildings in the centre have been knocked down. We can rest in the bus shelter built there, catch a bus to Hull or York or go into the Bay Horse for a well earned drink!

Market Place, Penny Bun.

Linegate, showing Garden Place.

Garden Place. Now Powell and Young's car park.

The Market Hill and Market Place.

ACTIVITIES

Fancy dress, about 1900.

Coronation of King George V.

Harold Lyon presenting a shield at the show.

Methodist Garden Party at Ashfield.

Planting a Coronation Tree (1911?)

Market Weighton Show, 1909.

Market Weighton Tennis Club.

Thomas G. Lyon planting tree on The Green.

The service for VE day, 50 years on, at St. John's.

The Royal car passing through York Road, on the Jubilee tour.

VILLAGES

Bladon's removals, 1913.

Cliffe Church, 1911

Goodmanham school, late 1920s.

Londesborough cricket team. Possibly during wartime.

Newbald Baptists' trip

Park Farm, Holme, 1915

Sancton

Shipton cricket team.

BIBLIOGRAPHY

Aldabella, P. and Barnard, R., *Hull and East Yorkshire Breweries,* (1997).

Bellingham, R., 'Early Telephone Subscribers in Pocklington', *East Yorkshire Local History Bulletin No. 51*, (1994-5).

Cox A. G. and Stather, D., *History of the Parish,* (1957).

East Riding Directories from 1823.

Gregory, R., *East Yorkshire Windmills,* (1985).

Ladley, G. P., *Centenary of the Building of the Present [St. John's] Chapel, (1968).*

Neave, D. R., *Londesborough,* (1977).

Neave, D. R., *Market Weighton Portrayed,* (1981).

Neave, D. R. and S., *East Riding Chapels and Meeting Houses,* (1990).

Up The Hill, (1960-1).

Wright, B., *The British Fire Mark 1680-1879,* (1982).

Tel-el-Fara, Londesborough Road.

FOR THE LOAN OF PHOTOGRAPHS

Jean Atkinson
Kathleen Briggs
William Copeland
Alwyn Davis
Doreen Emmerson
Joan Johnson
Harry and Mary Martin
Bruce Miles
Elaine Miles
Eva Playforth
John and Joan Speak
Mabel Swales
David Waby
Joyce White
Jim and Eileen Wilson
John Wregghitt for loan of the Parkinson photographic collection.
Doris Wright
John Moore for the loan of the Oddfellows Hall deeds
Peter Plantenga for sight of deeds of the Floral Hall
Colin Dyson for sight of the deeds of his jeweller's shop
Bruce Miles for index of deeds of Cooper's shop.

INFORMATION FROM

I wish to acknowledge with gratitude:
Roger Bellingham
Robert Jackson of Yorkshire Electricity, Goole.
Kenneth O. M. Kolisti
Ivan Medforth
Ethel Malyon
John Morfin for his chapter on the Market Weighton railway.
Kathleen Newbury
Joan Scalway
Audrey Sugden
The staff of the Beverley Reference Library
The staff of the East Riding of Yorkshire Archives
The staff of the Borthwick Institute
The staff of the Hull Local Studies Library
The staff of the York City Reference Library
The staff of the York Minster Library
The staff of Driffield Library
Market Weighton Town Council
Mr Bryan Dyson, Archivist at Brynmor Jones Library, Hull University – and others who have helped in many different ways.

All the people and businesses that have endured my visits to take photographs.

The encouragement of many people to battle on.

The old White House, Northgate, now demolished.

INDEX

Maypole on the Green.

St. Catherine's Nursing Home, Londesborough Road.